Mary Rose's 1001 Country Household Hints

=Mary Rose's=
1001 COUNTRY
HOUSEHOLD HINTS
=Mary Rose Quigg=

SELECT
EDITIONS

ISBN 1-84406-007-1

Line illustrations by Zöe Short.

Printed in China

First published in 1990 by David & Charles plc.

This edition published 2003 by
.TAJ BOOKS Ltd 27 Ferndown
Gardens Cobham Surrey
KT11 2BH.

For Selectabook Ltd., Roundway, Devizes,
Wiltshire, SN10 2 H T

Reprinted 1997,1998,1999,2000,2001,2002,2003,2004.
2005.

*C*ONTENTS

$\mathcal{A}$CKNOWLEDGEMENTS

※　※　※　※　※

I would like to extend my thanks to friend and mentor André Jute, who was instrumental in the publication of this book, and to Michael Keating and all friends who gave me assistance. I am also indebted to my mother, Mary Heron, for donating her cache of hints. And, of course, my special thanks to Joe and the children for their support and encouragement.

$\mathcal{I}$NTRODUCTION

We are all guilty of crime – the crime of not living life to the full.

HENRY MILLER

If, like many people in today's hectic world, you yearn for the more leisured pace of a gentler age, but find instead that an apparently infinite list of tasks has to be fitted into an ever-diminishing domestic day, then this is the book for you: a comprehensive collection of over a thousand invaluable hints and tips.

Traditional country hints have been tried, tested and passed down from generation to generation, in some cases for hundreds of years. Their purpose is simply to improve the quality of daily life for everyone involved in the domestic round, so that day-to-day tasks can be completed efficiently and enjoyably and still leave plenty of time for the many other facets of family life.

Over my many years as a busy country housewife and mother of five boisterous children, I have accumulated literally hundreds of indispensable household hints and tips. Many have been handed down through family and friends; some are the product of my own (sometimes bitter) experience; others are just plain common sense – but all give invaluable practical advice which, at some time or another, has helped our own household to run happily and smoothly.

In today's hectic (and expensive) world, ideas on how to save both time and money are always welcome, and you will find a wide range in the pages that follow. Thrifty housewives have always been aware of the value of recycling, but the hints and tips included in this book should help you develop it into something of an art, appropriate to the increasingly 'green' society in which we live. In fact, the emphasis throughout is on using natural products wherever appropriate – for everything from removing apparently impossible stains from a favourite carpet, to concocting your own polishes and shampoos (some old wives' tales really do contain more than a grain of truth) – so you can rest assured that your own home, at least, is as environment-friendly as possible.

7

Alongside practical advice on cooking, cleaning, decorating and DIY, needlework, gardening, health and beauty, and much more besides, I have included a sprinkling of apposite sayings, proverbs and poems – both traditional and not-so-traditional – that have not only given me great pleasure over the years, but also capture the flavour of life as perhaps it should be lived.

Compiling this book, sifting and sorting the vast treasure trove of hints, tips and ideas, has been a labour of love, as well as a positive pleasure. I hope you will find it both helpful and practical – and enduringly entertaining.

MARY ROSE

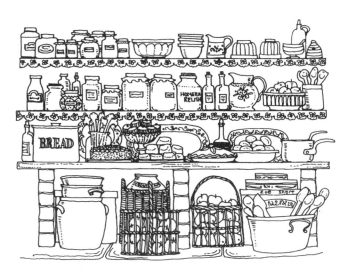

COOKERY CONSCIOUS

LOVER'S WEDDING CAKE

> *6lb flour of love*
> *1lb buttered youth*
> *1lb good looks*
> *1lb sweet temper*
> *1lb self-forgetfulness*
> *1oz dry humour*
> *3 tbsp rippling laughter*
> *2 wineglasses full of common sense*

Put flour of love, good looks and sweet temper into a well furnished home. Beat the butter of youth to a cream, mix together with kindness of faults, forgetfulness, powdered wit and dry humour into sweet argument. Then add to the rest of the ingredients. Pour in the rippling laughter and common sense. Work all together until well mixed. Bake gently forever.

9

COOKERY TIPS

As most recipes call for salt and pepper seasoning, keep a shaker filled with a mixture – three-quarters salt to one quarter pepper to save time.

Salt will keep dry and flow freely if kept in the refrigerator.

For a smooth mixture, add warm milk instead of cold when making white sauce.

If the milk boils over, sprinkle plenty of salt on it immediately and brush off; this eliminates that awful burning smell.

A substitute for salad cream – stir a little paprika and lemon juice into a carton of plain yogurt.

When making sandwiches for a party, pour ½pt (1¼ cups/275ml) boiling milk over 1lb (2 cups/450g) butter in a large basin. Cool and beat well until creamy. This mixture will spread easily.

To keep sandwiches fresh and moist, cover first with greaseproof paper, then with a cold, damp cloth.

Bread will keep up to three weeks in a fridge if wrapped in foil and put on a low shelf.

To cut bread really thin, keep dipping the knife into very hot water and dry before using.

For crisp fried bread – spread with butter or margarine and fry in a dry pan until golden brown on both sides.

Make golden crumbs for rissoles by crushing cornflakes.

Use coconut mixed with breadcrumbs to coat chicken pieces and rissoles – an unusual taste.

The critical period in matrimony is breakfast time.
A. P. HERBERT

COOKING WITH LEMONS

An average-sized lemon gives about 3tbsp (60ml) of juice.

A good-sized orange yields about 5tbsp (100ml) of juice.

When using the juice only of lemons or oranges, save the rind, grate finely and either dry in the oven or blend with caster sugar. Store in airtight jars or in the freezer.

When only a small drop of lemon juice is required, pierce the rind with a knitting needle and squeeze out what is needed. The rind will seal up again.

Add a squeeze of lemon juice to:

Mushrooms when frying, to bring out the flavour.
The water, to remove the smell, when cooking whole onions, cabbage or cauliflower.
Single cream to make sour cream.
The pan when tossing cooked cabbage or greens in butter.
Fresh milk to make it sour for baking.

Rub lemon juice over chicken skin before roasting to make crisp.

Before grating lemons, run the grater under the cold tap and the gratings will slip off easily.

When frying fish add 1tsp (5ml) lemon juice to the fat. This will improve the taste and make the pan easier to clean.

Lemon juice helps to keep fish white during cooking. Squeeze on an oily fish such as mackerel during grilling.

Keep sweetcorn yellow by adding 1tsp (5ml) lemon juice to the unsalted cooking water a minute before removing it from the heat. Salted cooking water toughens corn.

Keep poached eggs firm – add a little lemon juice to the water.

Always remember that the future comes one day at a time.

11

BEEF AND LAMB

To thaw frozen meat quickly, immerse it in cold water with a handful of salt, soak for 20min, rinse and pat dry.

When making Shepherd's Pie, finely crush three or four cheese flavoured biscuits and sprinkle them over the mashed potato.

One handful of medium oatmeal cooked with ½lb (1 cup/225g) raw minced beef will help the meat go further.

Hamburgers will cook more quickly if you poke a hole in the centre while shaping. When cooked, the hole will disappear.

Before using a pot for boiling meat or bacon joints, place some cooking foil on the bottom to prevent the meat from sticking.

To tenderise tough meat, add 1tbsp (20ml) vinegar to the cooking water. For steak, rub in a mixture of malt vinegar and cooking oil and allow to stand for two hours.

When grilling (broiling) meat on a rack, place a slice of bread in the grill pan. This eliminates smoking fat and reduces the fire risk.

If you have to keep beef or lamb in the fridge for a few days, rub it all over with vinegar and sprinkle with chopped onion. Wipe off the onion before cooking.

Before roasting lamb, tuck bits of garlic into tiny holes in the meat to improve the flavour.

To remove excess fat from stock, drop ice cubes into the pot and the fat will cling to the cubes. If you have no fridge then place a few lettuce leaves in the pot and watch the fat cling to them.

For a smooth gravy, keep a jar of equal parts flour and cornflour. Put 3 to 4tbsp (60 to 80ml) of this mixture into another jar, add some water and shake well – add the smooth paste to your gravy.

Friends are lost by calling often and calling seldom.

Recognise Good Quality Beef

1. Meat should be firm to the touch.

2. The lean should be bright red with a brownish tinge. Dark coloured meat with a dry appearance usually indicates that it is from an old or inferior animal, or that the meat has been cut and exposed to the air for some time.

3. The fat should be a cream colour. Sometimes it can be almost yellow and this is due to certain breeding and feeding.

4. The flesh should contain small flecks of fat giving a 'marbling' effect. This produces tenderness in cooking. The outside fat is no substitute for this. Very lean meat can be tough and flavourless.

5. A layer of gristle between the muscle and the outer layer of fat indicates an old animal. The amount of visible gristle varies with the cut, but prime cuts should contain very little.

Recognise Good Quality Lamb

1. The colour of the flesh will vary from light pink in a young lamb to a light or dark red, depending on the breed and age of the sheep.

2. In the spring and early summer the fat should be white and firm.

3. Brittle white indicates that the lamb has been too long in the freezer. Yellowish fat shows age. However, if longer and slower methods of cooking are used with these joints, they have good flavour, but quite a strong taste.

4. A layer of fat should cover the legs and shoulder, and they should look plump. A blue tinge in the knuckle bones and a lighter coloured flesh indicates that the animal is young.

Too many cooks spoil the broth.

PORK AND POULTRY

To make stock from meat bones, brown them first under a hot grill and the stock will have a deep rich colour.

For more tender liver, steep in milk for 30min before cooking.

Before frying sausages, dip them in milk, then roll in plain flour. This gives them a tasty crust and helps prevent sticking.

Fasten frying sausages together with skewers for easy turning.

Improve the flavour of pork chops – quickly brown them in a hot pan with a little fat, add a cupful of strained grapefruit juice. Simmer gently for 40min.

Baste a pork joint or chops with cider or pineapple juice. This improves the flavour and gives the meat a rich golden appearance.

When making stuffing for pork, grate an apple in to it.

Guarantee good crackling on your pork without overcooking by rubbing salt well into the scored skin (cuts close together). Leave overnight, then wipe off and rub the skin with cooking oil before putting into the oven.

To prevent white meat from discolouring during cooking, add a few drops of lemon juice or a dessertspoonful (10ml) of vinegar to the water.

After flouring chicken, chill for one hour. The coating adheres better during frying.

Roasted broiler chicken will taste more like a free range bird if it is cooked with tarragon. Mash 1tbsp (2g) of the dry herb with a large knob of butter and seasoning and put into the cavity. Baste with the melted butter during cooking.

Allow a hot roast bird to stand covered with foil for 10min before carving. The juices settle and it carves more easily.

A good manager looks ahead.

Recognise Good Quality Pork

1. The meat should be firm and smooth to touch, with little or no gristle. Older animals will have more gristle than young ones.

2. The colour of the flesh varies according to the age:

   young animals – pink with a fine texture
   older animals – a deeper pink or rose colour
   very old – dark red and coarse grained.

A brownish dry look indicates either poor quality or staleness.

3. Cut surfaces should be slightly moist to the touch but not wet with fluid.

4. The flesh should have small flecks of fat through it, a 'marbling ' effect to increase flavour and tenderness.

5. The fat on well-fed animals will be white and firm. Poor quality may be greyish or soft and oily looking. A good layer of outside fat shows good quality and feeding.

6. In a young animal the skin or rind should be thin and elastic, but it is rough and thick in an old one.

7. Bones should be small, fine and pinkish in a young animal, becoming off-white with age.

Recognise Good Quality Poultry

1. The only indication of quality in oven-ready birds is their plumpness and colour. Fresh or de-frosted poultry have a white skin.

2. When sold with feet and head on, young birds can be known by their smooth feet and legs and flexible beaks.

3. Young geese and ducks have a pliable under bill.

4. A young turkey has smooth back legs.

One party that always ends up in the kitchen is the hostess.

MARY BURDEN

FISH

When skinning fish, dip your fingers in water and then in salt to grip the skin and prevent the fish slipping.

To cook sprats without frying, roll them in seasoned flour and then thread them on to metal skewers. Place in a greased tin and cook for 20min in a hot oven.

When grilling kippers, put 1 to 2tbsp (20 to 40ml) water under them and they will keep moist in the steam.

Frying fish – sprinkle a little curry powder into the pan. It stops the smell and improves the flavour and colour.

Try flavouring your fish with orange juice instead of lemon.

Crush a packet of potato crisps and mix with grated cheese. Put on top of a dish of fish baked in milk. Grill before serving.

For a tasty coating on fish, spread salad cream on it instead of the usual egg before dipping in breadcrumbs.

Thaw frozen fish in milk – it removes the stale frozen taste and provides a 'fresh caught' flavour.

To rid tinned shrimp of its 'tinned' taste, soak in a little sherry and 2tbsp (40ml) vinegar for about 15min.

Add a few drops of vinegar when cooking white fish. This improves the texture and keeps fish a good colour.

Add white wine or finely sliced carrot, herbs and seasoning, to the water or stock to improve the flavour when cooking fish.

Dip fish in beaten egg, then in crushed cornflakes – a nice change from breadcrumbs.

Towers are measured by their shadows.

VEGETABLES

Potatoes

Soak new potatoes for 10min in hot water with a little baking soda and they will be easier to scrape. Or soak in salted water.

Keep new scraped potatoes without discolouration, for several hours, by covering in water with a few tablespoonsful of milk added.

Drain boiled new potatoes, cover with a clean tea towel for 2min. This absorbs excess moisture and makes them floury.

Old potatoes, which tend to go black, will remain a good colour if 1tsp (5ml) vinegar or lemon juice is added to the water halfway through cooking time.

A sprig or two of mint added to old potatoes for the last 5min of cooking will improve their flavour.

1tsp (5g) sugar dropped into boiling potatoes improves the flavour and makes them floury.

VEGETABLES

Add a little milk to the cooking water when boiling peeled potatoes to keep them white. For extra special creamed potatoes, cook in milk, drain, add salt and pepper, ¼tsp (1g) baking soda and a knob of butter before mashing.

Overcooked mashed potatoes become soggy if milk is added, instead sprinkle them with dry powdered milk.

To keep cooked potato hot for 15min – drain the pot and cover with a piece of cheese cloth.

Make neat potato salad by cutting the raw potato into small cubes. Place in a deep-fry basket in boiling water and cook gently until soft. Drain well and cool.

Before frying cold cooked potatoes, slice and dredge them with flour and place in very hot fat. They will brown quickly and have a better flavour.

After cutting potatoes into chips, soak them in cold water a few minutes, then dry on a clean tea towel before frying. This removes the excess starch, prevents chips sticking together and makes them crisper.

Add bacon rind to the chip pan when making chips to give them a bacony flavour. Or lay an onion on top of the cooking chips for additional flavour.

When frying chips throw in diced carrots or any root vegetable for variety.

Before baking potatoes soak them in boiling water for 15min. Dry and brush skin with cooking oil to speed up cooking.

Potatoes will bake in half the time if you push a skewer through them. The skewer acts as a heat conductor.

Before roasting potatoes, remove the centre with a corer. Push a small tightly rolled piece of bacon into the hole.

Optimists are wrong just as often as pessimists but they have a much happier time.

For crispy roast potatoes – first bring to the boil in well salted water, drain and sprinkle liberally with flour. Put into a hot pan in which the meat is roasting and continue as usual.

If food has been over-salted, cut a fairly large potato into slices, add to the pan, and cook a little longer. Potatoes absorb salt.

Remove root vegetables from plastic bags when storing or they will sweat and sprout.

Peel root vegetables thinly as most of the minerals and vitamins lie just beneath the skin.

Onions and Mushrooms

When peeling onions, soak in cold water for half an hour before peeling to prevent irritation to the eyes. Alternatively, peel under a running cold tap.

Soak onion rings in milk, drain well before frying in hot vegetable oil and they will be tasty and crisp.

Fried onions will be brown and crisp if first dipped in egg-white or evaporated milk. Drain, coat lightly with flour and fry quickly in hot fat.

Keep boiled onions whole while cooking by cutting a small cross at the stem of each one. Or make a hole through the centre of the onion with a skewer.

When boiling onions to be served whole, cook in a wire basket in the water for easy removal.

Forgiveness and a smile is the best revenge.

VEGETABLES

Place any unused portion of onion in a screwtop jar in the fridge – it will keep fresh for several days.

Refrigerate or freeze an onion before grating it for soup.

After chopping onions, rub your hands with a little sugar or dry mustard. Then wash with warm water and soap, rinse and dry.

Store mushrooms in the door of the fridge, not the coldest part.

Use an egg-slicer to chop mushrooms.

Mushrooms won't shrink in the frying pan if you pour boiling water over them beforehand.

Mushrooms will taste better if you sprinkle them with lemon juice and a little salt, then leave for a few minutes before cooking.

Add chopped mushroom stalks to meat pies, casseroles, and soups for additional flavouring.

Whatever women do, they must do twice as well as men, to be thought half as good. Luckily this is not difficult.
CHARLOTTE WHITTON

SALAD VEGETABLES

To improve salads – cut a garlic clove and rub the inside of the salad bowl with the cut surface – it gives a subtle garlic flavour.

To make celery curls, cut celery into 2in (5cm) pieces, cut in thin horizontal strips. Leave in cold water 30min to curl.

Celery leaves dried on a cake rack in a very slow oven are ideal for flavouring soups and stews.

Lettuce and celery keep longer if stored in the fridge in paper. Do not remove the outer leaves until ready to use.

Crisp limp lettuce and celery by placing in a pan of cold water for an hour with slices of raw potato, or a piece of washed coal.

Lettuce leaves will be crisper if a little vinegar is added to the washing water. This also helps to remove insects and sand.

Open a tight lettuce heart without breaking the leaves by holding it under a running cold tap.

Make soft tomatoes firm again by placing in salted iced water.

To peel tomatoes, place tomato on a kitchen fork and hold over high gas jet until skin 'pops'. Keep turning. Or put tomatoes in basin, cover with boiling water. Remove after half a minute.

To make tomato water-lilies: make zigzag cuts (7 points) through the centre of the tomato using a sharp knife. Pull halves apart gently.

To make carrot curls – choose a large carrot. Remove thin slices with a potato peeler. Curl and skewer with a pin. Leave in cold water until required. Remove pin before serving.

It takes four men to make a salad dressing: a generous one for the oil, a miser for the vinegar, a wise man for the salt, and a madman for the pepper.

OTHER VEGETABLE HINTS

To chop parsley quickly, put a few sprigs in a teacup, snip with kitchen scissors, turning the cup as you work.

Chew a piece of parsley after eating garlic to remove the smell from your breath.

Garlic cloves will never dry out if stored in a bottle of cooking oil. After the stored garlic is used, use the flavoured oil for salad dressing.

Rub stale bread slices with garlic, cut into cubes, fry in butter to serve with soup or use with salad.

When cauliflower has gone a little brown, 1tsp (5ml) milk added to the boiling water returns it to its fresh white colour.

Keep cabbage and cauliflower stumps – grate and mix with grated onion and mayonnaise for an inexpensive coleslaw.

Keep cabbage green by putting it in a perforated plastic bag and hanging it outdoors.

A few strips of raw bacon rind tied together with thread and added to boiling cabbage adds a delicious flavour.

A large piece of parsley placed in the saucepan when cooking cabbage or brussels sprouts will minimise any odour. Or add a few bay leaves to the boiling water before adding the vegetables. This does not affect their flavour.

For a spicy taste to your food – drain boiled cabbage and sprinkle with a little dry curry powder.

When cooking peas add celery salt instead of ordinary salt.

Never overcook vegetables, boil until tender, drain well and serve.

A vegetable is a substance used to balance a child's plate while it's being carried to and from the kitchen.

Use an egg-slicer to slice cooked beetroot for pickling.

Stand stuffed tomatoes and peppers in patty-pans before baking them and they'll hold their shape better.

For a change from fried tomato, peel, core and slice an apple and fry it with bacon.

Add a few pieces of bacon rind to bought tomato soup while heating and this will enhance the flavour. Remove before serving.

Make your own curried beans by stirring 1tsp (5ml) concentrated curry sauce and some raisins into a large tin of baked beans.

When cooking frozen beans, place in a colander over a saucepan already in use, and steam for 10min.

Restore a 'fresh flavour' to frozen vegetables by pouring boiling water over them and rinsing away the traces of the frozen water.

Make up purees of cooked mixed root vegetables such as parsnip and carrot; swede and celeriac; potato, horseradish and yogurt; soured cream and spices, to make tasty accompaniments.

Use an electric hand mixer to mash potatoes and vegetables.

Some root vegetables such as carrots, onions or turnips have natural sweetness. To enhance this, add a pinch of sugar or orange juice while cooking.

Avoid using turnips for soups, stews, stock, etc, which you are not using the same day. Turnips go 'off' more quickly than other vegetables.

When peeling root vegetables, add a handful of salt to the water to prevent your hands becoming stained.

A food is not necessarily essential just because your child hates it.
KATHERINE WHITEHORN

THE INVALUABLE EGG

When checking the freshness of an egg remember:

> they should be heavy, for size
> they should have a rough shell
> if you break an egg on a plate, the yolk should be high and rounded, and the white should be jelly-like.

When using eggs:

> Use at room temperature. Remove from the fridge about an hour before use.
> Cold eggs will be more likely to crack when boiled, curdle when cooked and not whip as well.
> Cook gently – rapid cooking causes curdling and toughness.
> Cool hot mixtures before adding to egg.
> Before whisking egg-whites make sure that the bowl, beaters, etc, are free from any trace of fat or the whites will not whisk well.
> When separating eggs, make sure there is no yolk in the white as the whisked volume will be less.

Did you know that the colour of the shell or yolk of an egg has nothing to do with its food value?

If eggs are stuck to the carton, just wet the box and the eggs are easily removed.

Never wash eggs – this removes their natural protective coating.

Make scrambled eggs in a buttered basin over a pan of hot water. The scramble will be creamier and there will be no messy pan to clean.

Scrambled egg can be varied by adding a handful of crushed potato crisps when cooking.

Enough is better than too much.

24

An omelette will be lighter if you add a dessertspoonful (10ml) of water, not milk, for every egg. Do not overbeat.

For fluffier omelettes add a pinch of cornflour before beating.

To cook an omelette, use half cooking oil and half butter as this is less likely to stick than all butter.

Put a spent match in the water when boiling eggs; if they should crack the contents will stay intact. Or add a little vinegar.

When hard-boiling eggs, heat the water before you add the eggs so that around the yolks won't turn black. Dip the knife in boiling water when slicing eggs and the slices won't crumble.

Plunge hard-boiled eggs immediately after cooking into cold water and crack the shells. Take out and place in the fridge until required. The shells will peel off easily.

A potato masher is useful when mixing several hard-boiled eggs for sandwiches. Add butter, pepper and salt then mash well for a creamy mixture that will spread easily.

When separating the yolk of an egg from the white, break the egg into a pie funnel. The yolk remains intact while the white runs through.

To make egg whites thicken up faster, add a pinch of salt before beating.

Add one whisked egg-white to a carton of double cream to double the quantity.

To keep spare egg-whites, put in a lidded jar in the fridge and use for meringues within two weeks. If you lose count of how many egg-whites are in the jar – four egg whites are about ¼pt (⅔cup/150ml).

To keep egg-yolks fresh, cover with cold water.

Hope is a good breakfast, but an ill supper.
FRANCIS BACON

BAKING TIPS

Butter cream will keep for up to three weeks in a covered container in the fridge. Make up a large quantity without flavourings and add them as required.

Use a spare eye-dropper to dispense food colouring or flavouring.

If icing sugar has hardened, place it in the bread bin for a few days and it will soften.

Don't waste left-over royal icing – make peppermint creams by adding more icing sugar and a few drops of peppermint essence until you get a pliable soft consistency. Roll out and cut into circles with a bottle top.

To soften solid lumps of sugar and speed up creaming of butter and sugar – place in the microwave for a few seconds.

Soft brown sugar often goes hard when stored. To soften it – place in a bowl and cover with a fairly damp tea towel for a few hours. If needed in a hurry, grate the hard block of sugar.

To keep pancakes soft, beat 1oz (30g) melted butter into the batter.

Add a dessertspoonful (10g) of ground rice to the flour when making pudding batter; it will make the pudding lighter.

To make Yorkshire puddings rise well, use half milk and water instead of all milk.

Warm nuts for 30min in a low oven or soak in cold salted water overnight – crack carefully and the kernels will stay whole.

To blanch almonds, place whole almonds in a basin and pour boiling water over them. Leave for 5min. Drain. The skin will come off easily by pinching between the finger and thumb.

Cooks are not to be taught in their own kitchens.

Treacle or golden syrup will leave the spoon more readily if you heat the spoon beforehand.

To measure golden syrup, cover the scale pan with flour; the syrup will tip out quite easily.

To remove the syrup from glacé cherries before using, put into a sieve and rinse under running water. Drain well and dry thoroughly with kitchen paper.

A substitute for ground almond is ground rice flavoured with almond essence.

For a more tasty pastry, add 1tsp (5g) ground almond to pastry mix for mince pies.

For a very light shortcrust pastry use soda water instead of tap water.

When making pastry in hot weather or a warm kitchen – use fat straight from the fridge, hold your wrists under the cold tap before you start, and place the dough in the fridge for at least 30min before rolling out.

Before making a flan or quiche, cut two strips of greaseproof paper about 2in (5cm) wide. Lay at right angles across the baking tin and leave the ends projecting. Use these handles to lift out the cooked flan later.

Sprinkle a covering of white breadcrumbs at the bottom of fruit pies before adding fruit to prevent pastry becoming soggy. Or save biscuit crumbs from the tin and use them.

When steaming Christmas puddings, put the bowls inside roasting bags with the top open to avoid getting burnt fingers when removing them from the hot water.

Before using citrus fruits, pare off the rind with a potato peeler, cut into small pieces, put in a screwtop jar, cover with golden syrup and mix well. Delicious if added to cakes.

Put orange peel on a plate in the oven and leave till crisp. Then crush to powder and store in a jar. Small amounts added to cake mixtures give a lovely flavour.

Clear as you go: muddle makes muddle.

BAKING TIPS

Put dates through a mincer before making a date loaf. This ensures a moist loaf and a more even distribution of the fruit.

When raisins become hard, put them in a colander over a saucepan of nearly boiling water. After a few minutes the steam makes them plump and juicy again.

Make your own shortbread in the usual way, then melt a Mars Bar and spread over the top. Leave to harden before slicing.

When plain biscuits go soft, place a chocolate drop on each one, put in a low oven for 10min for crisp chocolate biscuits.

When melting chocolate, place it in a stainless steel jug in the oven with buns or cake and it will be ready when they are cooked. It also helps to grease the sides and bottom of the container as this prevents sticking and waste.

After a baking session, rinse floury basins, cutlery or board first in cold water. Hot water makes flour more difficult to remove.

Take away the fuel and you take away the fire.

CONJURE UP A CAKE

Greaseproof or butter paper is excellent for lining cake tins.

For a rich fruit cake, half plain and half self-raising flour gives a better result.

Three days before you mix the Christmas cake, put the dried fruit into a screwtop jar and pour the alcohol over it. Seal and turn it over every twelve hours.

To be certain that cake tins have equal amounts of mixture, weigh tins when filled and balance the quantity so that they are equal.

A bowl of water placed in an electric oven will help keep a rich fruit cake moist.

If a cake is inclined to stick to the tin – stand the tin on a damp cloth for a few minutes.

Slice stale fruit cake thinly, dampen with sherry and bake between thin layers of pastry. Cut into squares.

To keep a fruit cake moist, place in an airtight tin with a sound apple.

Before putting a cake into the freezer, cut it into slices and place in separate bags. Then you can remove as much as you require.

An easy way to fill an icing bag is to put the empty bag inside a jug or glass and fold the bag over the top edge, then fill.

To make a quick and unusual icing – dissolve a few jelly cubes in some hot water and mix with icing sugar. Alternatively use orange squash instead of water – the result is tasty and sets quickly.

Icing sets more quickly if mixed with a little boiling water.

Heat the blade of the knife in boiling water before cutting an iced cake – it gives a clean cut without breaking the icing.

Eat at pleasure, drink by measure.

CONJURE UP A CAKE

When baking cakes or bread:

Prepare the tin before you start – grease and/or line it.
Pre-heat the oven to the correct temperature.
Weigh all the ingredients accurately. The amount of raising agent is vital to the success of a recipe.
Use fresh ingredients.
Sieve flour and raising agent together to mix well.
The correct consistency is very important.
Once mixture is moistened do not delay before baking.
Most cakes are baked in the centre of the oven.
Avoid opening the oven door during the first 10min of cooking.
Time baking accurately.
Test to see if it's done before removing from the oven.
Cool on a wire tray.

For a lighter and tastier sponge fold 1tsp (20ml) boiling water into the mixture before baking.

To test a sponge, press lightly with thumb on centre of cake. If ready, it will spring back immediately. The sides of the cake will have shrunk from the tin. Also, listen to the cake, if you can hear it gently sizzling, it is not quite done.

Warm jam before spreading on a sponge, then it will not soak in.

For a different cake topping, cover a newly baked sponge with chocolate peppermint creams. Return to the oven for about a minute to melt, then spread evenly.

An unusual sandwich cake filling is a layer of orange marmalade, covered with a layer of peanut butter. Top with orange icing.

To make sure of a straight edge when trimming a cake, place the cake on a flat surface and, using a sharp serrated-edged knife, cut with one movement using a cake ruler as a guide.

It's an ill cook that cannot lick his own fingers.

DESSERT TOPPINGS

Add a sliced banana to the white of an egg and beat until stiff. The banana will disappear and you'll have a lovely change from whipped cream.

Whip up an egg-white, gradually add a little syrup, stirring until the mixture is thick and creamy. Delicious served with fruit.

Gently melt a few peppermint creams and pour over vanilla ice-cream to make a delicious sweet.

Make a quick, sweet sauce topping by cutting up a bar of fudge and melting it with 1tbsp (20ml) hot water. Add some chopped nuts and glacé cherries. Serve with ice-cream and desserts.

A sauce for fruit salad can be made by whipping a small carton of double cream until thick, add 2tbsp (40ml) honey before mixing with 1tbsp (20ml) lemon juice.

Whip cream with honey instead of sugar – it stays firmer longer.

Spoon natural yogurt sweetened with honey over fruit pies and crumbles instead of custard or cream.

When making custard, use moist brown sugar instead of white – it gives a caramel flavour.

Add a pinch of salt when boiling milk for making custard. This gives it the 'ice-cream' taste that children love.

Prevent skin forming on custard by sprinkling with sugar before it cools.

A quick and easy way to make lemon sauce to serve with steamed ginger sponge – add a dessertspoonful (10ml) of lemon curd to 1pt (2½ cups/550ml) of white sauce and stir well.

Subdue your appetites my dears and you've conquered human nature.

CHARLES DICKENS

FRUITS OF THE SEASON

When stewing apples use less sugar and add 1tsp (5ml) syrup.

To keep fruit whole when stewing, always bring the water or syrup to the boil before adding the fruit, then simmer gently.

Try grating a cooking apple into the mixture when making bread and butter pudding, for a different flavour.

Slice apples into slightly salted water when preparing them for cooking – this prevents browning.

Make fruit crumble extra tasty – substitute bran for half the flour.

Sprinkle apple slices with plain flour when making a tart. As the apples soften, the flour acts as a thickening agent.

Soft brown sugar is better than white when stewing rhubarb. It gives a delicious caramel flavour and removes the tartness. Add a square of red jelly to give better colour.

Reduce the acidity of rhubarb by cooking it in cold tea.

When stewing rhubarb, add a few thin slices of lemon plus rind.

To skin grapes, plunge into boiling water for 2min, then cold water. The skins will come off easily.

Ripen green bananas or tomatoes by wrapping them in a wet dish cloth and placing them in a paper bag.

Enjoy fresh pineapple soon after purchase – don't store. A pineapple is ripe when the scent comes through the skin and the leaves should be stiff.

To freeze strawberries or raspberries, remove hulls, wash in ice cold water and dry thoroughly on a clean cloth. Open freeze on flat trays, then pack frozen without sugar, in polythene bags.

JAM-MAKING

Choose slightly under-ripe fruit rather than over-ripe. Prepare fruit, taking care to remove damaged or bruised pieces.

Rub the inside of the jam pan with butter, for easier cleaning.

Put the stones from stone-fruit in muslin, and cook in the jam to improve the flavour.

Granulated sugar is best. Caster sugar or brown sugar produce a lot of froth and are not recommended.

Warm the sugar for jam-making in a heat-proof bowl in a low oven while you are cooking the fruit. It will dissolve more quickly.

Cook the fruit thoroughly so that all the pectin is extracted before adding sugar.

After adding sugar, allow it time to dissolve completely before the jam starts to boil. Do not overstir jam.

When stirring, make a large figure of eight to prevent sticking.

Avoid over-boiling jam or it will be dark coloured and sugary.

To test if jam is at setting point – drop a teaspoonful onto an ice-cold plate and it should wrinkle when touched after a minute.

If jam will not set, reboil it with 2tbsp (40ml) fresh lemon juice or the recommended amount of pectin to each 4lb (2kg) of fruit.

When making marmalade, add 1pt (2½ cups/550ml) pineapple juice instead of water for a delicious flavour.

Cover jam while still hot and store in a dry, airy cupboard – not on a high kitchen shelf where rising heat may cause it to ferment.

If home-made jam becomes sugary, stand the jar in a saucepan of cold water and heat slowly. This will dissolve the sugar.

If you can't stand the heat, get out of the kitchen.

Enjoy a Snack

Cut up an apple into thin slices, place on buttered bread. Sprinkle with grated cheese and salted peanuts then grill (broil) until bubbling hot.

Toast a slice of bread on one side. On the other side spread sliced banana thinly, sprinkle with brown sugar and put under the grill.

Butter a slice of toast, top with a pineapple ring, fill the centre of the ring with grated cheese, then grill for a few minutes.

Make cinnamon toast by mixing 1tsp (5g) cinnamon to a heaped tablespoonful (30g) sugar. Shake on ordinary toast and keep warm in the oven until ready to use.

For a quick snack, cook button mushrooms in butter and cream and heap onto toast. Parsley and chives can be added if available.

Make a tin of salmon go further in sandwiches by grating some carrot into it.

A quick, nourishing snack is to melt a knob of butter on an enamel plate, remove from the heat and break an egg onto it, add a little salt and toss the egg, cook gently over a moderate heat.

Prepare a savoury pancake mix and divide into two bowls. Add grated potato to one and chopped mushrooms to the other, add herbs to both and season with garlic salt and pepper. Fry in hot fat to make a perfect accompaniment for any meal.

Poach haddock or cod fillets in milk, drain, cover with a mixture of a packet of crushed crisps and grated cheese. Bake in the oven for a few minutes.

Liven up a can of ordinary baked beans by adding 1tsp (5g) each of dry mustard and brown sugar, and 1tbsp (20ml) vinegar.

Fry a large sliced onion until tender, add to a can of beans in an ovenproof dish. Cover with layers of grated cheese, mashed potato and more cheese. Bake in a moderate oven for 15min.

Hunger finds no fault with the cooking.

Finely chop a small onion, grate 2oz (60g) cheese and one raw potato. Mix with one beaten egg and pour into a frying pan with hot fat or butter. Cook until golden.

Crumble 4oz (120g) of corned beef into 2lb (900g) of mashed potato. Add 2oz (60g) grated cheese and some tomato. Grill until the cheese melts.

Use left-over mashed potato for savoury croquettes by adding finely chopped onion, tomato, parsley and grated cheese. Mix well, form croquettes, roll in flour before frying.

To serve new potatoes – remove the skin, wash and boil in salted water. Drain and add chopped spring onion, 2oz (60g) butter and a heaped teaspoon (5g) of rolled oats. Toss all together in the pan.

Boil some large potatoes for about 10min, drain. Rub the skin with oil and prick with a fork. Bake until tender. Cut in half, scoop out the centres and mix this potato with cheese or tomato, or grilled bacon, sausage or any vegetables. Sprinkle with cheese and grill (broil).

Make a quick, cold sweet by spreading jam, syrup, stewed apples or sliced banana over the bottom of a flan case. Cover with thick custard and sprinkle with fine coconut.

For a delicious speedy sweet – slice a chocolate swiss roll, put a scoopful of ice-cream on each slice, cover with meringue and bake in a hot oven for a few minutes.

The main purpose of children's parties is to remind you
that there are children more awful than your own.

ＡROUND THE ＨOUSE

Around the house I dust and clean,
*   then I come upon a scene.*
A spider spinning a fragile web,
*   behind the headboard of the bed.*
Creating threads with skill and grace,
*   a beautiful trellis is formed in space.*
I leave it free to twirl and spin,
*   then a household fly soars in.*
Straight into the web of course he flies,
*   must free him before he dies.*
Depriving the spider of his trap and prey,
*   I brush the delicate cobweb away.*

MARY ROSE

MONEY SAVING IDEAS

If gummed labels or postage stamps stick together, cover with a sheet of thin paper and press lightly with a warm iron. They will separate easily and the gum will be unaffected.

Pipe tobacco will keep fresh and moist longer if stored in an airtight tin with a few potato peelings.

Wrap apparently dead batteries in tinfoil and leave in a moderate oven when baking and they will be useful again. A small battery should be left in 20min while larger ones need 30min.

When filling a hot water bottle for the first time, put a few drops of glycerine into the water. This will make the rubber more supple.

If the rubber band round an old carpet sweeper perishes and drops off, replace it with a band of self-adhesive draught excluder.

To make rubber gloves last longer – when new turn them inside out and stick a strip of sticking plaster across the top of each finger. This also protects your nails.

Rubber gloves will last much longer if rinsed in clear water after use; clip with a clothes peg and hang up when not in use.

Before throwing away worn rubber gloves, cut strips from the cuffs to make some strong and useful bands.

To make an inexpensive wallbrush for inaccessible corners – a child's toy sweeping brush taped to a length of cane is ideal. It's light and easily handled.

Make a lamp base by taking an attractively shaped bottle, stick on used postage stamps to cover it completely and, when the glue has dried, coat with clear varnish.

Look after the pennies, and the pounds will look after themselves.

Turn old wire lampshades into hanging plant holders – attach three short lengths of chain to the upside down frame.

Use an old fridge as a cupboard in your garden shed or garage; make sure any locks are removed.

Convert an old water bottle into a useful garden 'kneeler'. Cut off the neck, fill the bottle with torn rags or old tights and sew the ends together.

Keep used oil from the chip pan for greasing your garden tools.

Keep used solid emulsion trays to be used as seed trays.

The trough-shaped container you get with ready-pasted wallpaper is a good plant holder when covered with adhesive shelf covering.

Save the lids from dried milk tins, coat with enamel and use as coasters for glasses and mugs, or under small plant pots.

Don't throw away old plastic table covers. Keep the best parts for lining cupboard shelves in the kitchen.

A used washing-up liquid container with the top cut off makes a good sink side holder for brushes. It can be painted to match kitchen equipment.

Old nylon pan scrubbers can be unwound to give long lengths of very strong nylon cord.

Draw-string bags made from net curtains make excellent storage bags for vegetables. Hang them from hooks inside the cupboard.

MONEY SAVING IDEAS

Use plastic bags from the supermarket as bin liners.

Keep used clingfilm – it makes ideal tags for packages in the freezer. Cut into strips, twist and tie a small knot at each end.

Save any left-over pieces of carpet and use them to cover the tops of stools. Just cut them to size and stick on.

For table mats that have become a bit tatty, paste on a picture from an old calendar or glossy magazine. Finish off work with a coat of heat-resistant varnish. Makes mats as good as new.

Give your table mats a new lease of life by covering them with a frilled cover made from material to match your curtains.

Save waxed paper from cereal packets – cut into circles for covering home-made jam.

Before discarding cereal or soap packets, cut out all the large letters. Keep as an educational word-making pastime for children.

Make a spaghetti storage jar by taking two plastic mineral water bottles, cut the top off one and the bottom off the other to become the lid.

Bags for vacuum cleaners are expensive, so carefully unfold the end, empty the bag, refold and seal with sticky tape.

During the summer months rinse, fold flat and save all litre milk cartons; in the winter fill them with wet slack for your fire.

Save heat and money by putting sheets of aluminium foil behind wall radiators. Heat escapes into walls but foil reflects it back into the room.

Frugality and economy are home virtues without which no household can prosper.

MRS BEETON

When a coffee tabletop is badly marked, cover with holiday snapshots or coloured postcards and a sheet of heavy glass. Seal the gap between glass and table with transparent adhesive tape to prevent dust entering.

Cut the least worn parts of old corduroy jackets and trousers into squares and make into cushion covers. Use old tights as filling.

When cotton curtains shrink, buy a piece of toning or contrasting fringe about the depth of the shortage. Stitch to the bottom of the curtains and press – this gives a new lease of life.

Make a patchwork bathmat from the best bits of old bright towels.

Make inexpensive toilet bags for the whole family from one brightly coloured plastic tablecloth.

Save small net bags from packets of dried peas, fill with scraps of soap and fasten under the hot tap to give you a lovely soapy bath.

Soap will last much longer if you buy it and store in a dry place for some weeks before use. Press a piece of kitchen foil against the side that rests on the basin.

The cardboard bases of kitchen and toilet rolls make excellent firelighters.

Glue left-over cork tiles to a piece of hardboard and you'll have a long lasting bathmat. Cork tiles make good tablemats too.

Renew old wool blankets by dyeing them a bright colour in the washing machine or bath. Shake well while on the clothes line to make them fluffy. Bind the edges with satin blanket ribbon.

How often could things be remedied by a word. How often is it left unspoken.
NORMAN DOUGLAS

MONEY SAVING IDEAS

Instead of buying pram sheets, use a pillowcase on the mattress.

Use two-litre plastic ice-cream boxes for stacking cassette tapes. Decorate the lids with cut-outs of favourite singers.

If the paints in your child's paint box become hard, put a drop or two of glycerine on each square, close the lid and leave for a few hours – the paint becomes almost like new.

Use children's bedroom wallpaper for wrapping children's presents.

A cheap paste for youngsters to use – buy cold water paste, making sure it is not anti-fungal. Make up a quantity and put into empty roll-on deodorant bottles.

Blow up balloons and write children's names on them with felt tipped pens. Let the air out. Use them for Christmas stockings, at birthday parties, or send with a message as a party invitation.

Empty cardboard tubes from kitchen foil can be used to keep gift wrapping paper or other special papers from becoming creased. They are also useful for sending prints by post. Plastic tops from hairspray or deodorant tins make excellent covers for tube ends.

A corner cut from a used envelope, slipped over the last page you read makes an excellent book marker.

A good present to give an old or disabled person is a packet of notelets with a stamp on every envelope. They can keep in touch with friends and family at no extra cost.

Waste not, want not, but you won't be able to get into the attic.

When you buy a new dressing gown don't throw away the old one. Cut it at the waist, bind the sleeves and waist with decorative material and you have a cosy bed-jacket.

Coat straw beach hats and bags with clear varnish. It will stop the straw splitting and give longer life.

If you are at home during the day, fill a large flask with boiling water at breakfast time and then you'll have hot water for drinks without boiling the kettle.

Save fuel, and washing-up, when cooking for two or three people by cooking different vegetables, in tinfoil parcels, in one saucepan.

Reputation is commonly measured by the acre.

CLEANING IN THE KITCHEN

When going on holidays or away for a few days, cut a fresh lemon in half and leave it in the kitchen. The room will smell lovely and fresh on your return.

After washing a breadbin with soapy water, rinse and wipe the inside with a vinegar-moistened cloth to prevent bread becoming mouldy.

Whiten a discoloured wooden draining- or bread-board by scrubbing it daily with cold salt water. Work the way of the grain, rub with a cut lemon to bleach the wood, then dry outdoors if possible.

To keep a fish-board fresh, clean away the oily stains by washing with soapy water, then scrub with mustard powder. Leave for a few minutes and rinse off.

Remove the smell of fish or onion from your hands by dampening them and rubbing with salt. Wash and rinse.

Clean scraps of meat or onion from your mincer by passing a piece of stale bread through after use. This can be added to the dish to help to thicken the mixture.

To clean a grater, brush the wrong side with a toothbrush; also you can sharpen your grater with sandpaper.

Tea stains on plastic vacuum flask tops can easily be removed. Rub the affected area gently with salt moistened with a few drops of vinegar.

To clean a vacuum flask that hasn't been used for some time – put 1tbsp (20ml) vinegar and 1 level tsp (5g) salt into the flask and shake well. Rinse with clean water.

Freshen a vacuum flask by placing 2tsp (10g) baking soda in the empty flask and top up with nearly boiling water. Leave overnight, empty and wash in soapy water. Rinse with warm water.

People in glass houses shouldn't throw stones.

CLEANING GLASS

Remove ice on windows quickly by rubbing with a cloth moistened with ammonia; and to prevent the glass steaming over in winter, rub with a cloth moistened in glycerine, methylated spirits or undiluted washing-up liquid.

Old newspapers rolled into a pad are splendid for cleaning windows. They remove all smears and shine the glass.

Use hot vinegar on a rag to remove bird marks or dried paint splashes from windows. Clean frosted glass with warm water containing vinegar and polish with a lintless cloth.

To clean the green residue from the bottom of a vase, fill with a solution of biological washing powder or liquid and water, then let soak. Rinse well. A few drops of ammonia added to the rinsing water makes the glass really shine.

If household bleach fails to remove discolouration from inside a narrow-necked glass flower vase, bottle or decanter, fill the container with warm water and 2tsp (10g) of sand. Shake well and rinse. Repeat if necessary.

Crushed egg-shells and water make an excellent scourer for vases.

Rinse crystal glass in a weak solution of vinegar to make it sparkle. Use a plastic bowl to avoid chipping precious crystal.

Add some sugar to warm water when washing flower glasses that have become dull.

Use a little fabric conditioner in warm water to clean glass-topped tables, TV screens or stereo lids, then rub dry. This prevents dust settling on the surface.

After washing walls or glass doors wipe with a cloth sprinkled with vinegar to remove the soap film. Polish with a dry cloth.

A new broom sweeps clean, but the old one knows the corners.

CLEANING POTS AND PANS

Remove rust from cake tin corners by scouring with a raw potato dipped in cleaning powder.

Clean domestic tinware by rubbing powdered washing soda on the surface with a moistened screwed-up ball of newspaper. Wash well with warm water. Dry and polish like new with more newspaper.

The bottoms of barbecue pots and pans will stay bright if they are rubbed over with a cake of soap before you use them on an open fire. The smoke stains will vanish when washed.

Before using a frying pan, brush with a small amount of oil, add 3tbsp (60g) salt and heat gently for 3min. With a large pad of kitchen paper rub the salt around the pan then wipe off. This prevents sticking.

Some non-stick frying pans become very discoloured; don't use scourers, instead soak overnight in a mild solution of household bleach. Rinse well.

Clean a burnt pan by simmering onion skins in it for an hour. Leave overnight and the blackened particles will slide away. Or sprinkle with baking soda, adding just enough hot water to moisten. Leave to stand for several hours. Rinse off.

When an enamel pan is badly burnt, sprinkle with a mixture of 1tbsp (20g) salt and 2tbsp (40ml) lemon juice. Leave for half an hour, then rub gently with a fine wire scrubber or steel wool.

If an aluminium pan has become discoloured, boil some apple peel in it for a few minutes, then rinse and dry.

Avoid washing an omelette pan, wipe with kitchen paper.

If you line your grill pan with foil, it will be easy to clean and will be more efficient.

Rest breeds rust!

CLEANING THE COOKER

Pipe cleaners are marvellous for cleaning the burner holes on gas stoves, removing dust from the typewriter and from the telephone.

To clean the metal work-top of a gas cooker use an old nylon stocking dipped in undiluted washing-up liquid.

After cleaning the top of the cooker, dry well and wipe over with a cloth sprinkled with olive or corn oil.

After using the oven, put a saucerful of ammonia on the bottom rack while it is warm. Wipe over the inside of the oven next day and the grease will come off easily. Finish off with a cloth dipped in a paste made from baking soda and water.

A useful oven cleaner is made with a solution of 1tbsp (20g) baking soda to ½pt (1¼ cups/275ml) hot water. Simply wipe over the whole oven, glass door and shelves, close the door and forget. Keep this solution in a screwtop jar and shake before use. Old burnt marks gradually disappear.

Make oven cleaning a lighter chore by soaking all removable parts in biological detergent overnight. All deposits can be wiped off easily with very hot water.

To clean a glass oven door or badly stained glass ovenware, wipe with a damp cloth dipped in salt. Rinse after 10min.

To get rid of the smell of solvents from a newly cleaned oven, heat some lemon rind in the oven for about 20min, then open the door and continue cooking for another 15min.

Cover gravy or juice spills on the bottom of the oven with salt. Lift off the spillage when the oven cools.

Put casserole dishes on a tray in the oven for easy removal. Move the cooker or heavy furniture by putting sacking or an old rug underneath. Then slide without strain or scratching the floor.

Economy is frequently a way of spending money without getting any fun out of it.

CLEANING FRIDGES AND SINKS

Wrap frozen food in newspaper when defrosting the freezer.

To speed up the process of defrosting a freezer, use a hairdryer once the ice has started to melt.

A pair of laundry tongs with a piece of towelling fixed over each arm will reach those difficult corners of the defrosted freezer.

After defrosting the freezer, brush a little glycerine over the inside. Next time the ice will fall off in sheets and reduce defrosting time.

To keep the inside of the fridge fresh when you've finished cleaning, wipe it out with a little cold water containing baking soda.

If the ice-tray sticks in the ice-box, put a piece of aluminium foil underneath.

Silence that annoying dripping tap until the plumber comes by putting a piece of string around the end of the tap and allowing it to trail down to the centre of the sink. The water will flow down the string noiselessly.

To prevent waste pipes from freezing in winter, keep sink and bath plugs in place, especially at night. Repair dripping taps.

Clean the outlet of a sink or washbasin by filling a small polythene spray bottle with diluted bleach and spraying it into the outlet. Flush with warm soapy water to remove sediment.

When a sink or bath wastepipe becomes blocked, clear it by probing with a flexible curtain rod, then pour down a kettleful of boiling water and a handful of washing soda.

To clear a blocked sink, push down a handful of baking soda, followed by a cupful of vinegar. Leave for 1 hour and then pour down plenty of boiling water.

Nagging is the repetition of unpalatable truths.

DEALING WITH BROOMS, BINS AND ODOURS

Wash brooms and brushes regularly in warm soapy water containing ammonia or soda crystals, then rinse well in cold salted water to stiffen the bristles. Dry outdoors.

Wipe a dirty galvanised bucket with a rag dipped in paraffin, then wash with hot soapy water to remove grease. Rinse and dry.

Soak lintless dusters in a bucket containing equal parts of paraffin and vinegar. Drip dry out of doors and store in a polythene bag.

Sprinkle baking soda in the ashtray. It keeps down odour and extinguishes the cigarette immediately.

Kill household smells and have a fresh smelling house – put a few drops of wintergreen oil on a cotton ball. Place in a glass container. It will last for months and is as effective as room sprays.

If kitchen knives smell of fish or onion, plunge into the earth several times and then wash in soapy water.

Use parsley as a fly deterrent.

To keep flies and wasps away from dustbins, attach a pad of blotting paper soaked in disinfectant to the inside of the lid.

Counteract unpleasant dustbin smells in summer by sprinkling the inside generously with salt.

If ants are troublesome in the house, sprinkle a mixture of sugar and borax where they run, but don't use it if you have small children or pets. Instead use talcum powder, or put some turpentine or peppermint essence on cotton wool and block their entrance point.

Each generation imagines itself to be more intelligent than the one that went before, and wiser than the one that comes after it.

GEORGE ORWELL

KITCHEN STAINS

To remove tannin stains from a teapot, put in 2tsp (10g) washing soda, fill with boiling water. Leave overnight and rinse well next day.

To remove stains from inside a china or silver teapot – place 1tsp (5g) borax in the pot, fill with hot water and leave overnight. Use a small paintbrush to clean the spout. Rinse well.

To keep an unused teapot fresh – leave a dry tea-bag or sugar lump in it.

Boil a discoloured coffee pot for a short time in a strong solution of borax. Rinse thoroughly.

To make yellowing kitchen appliances white again, mix 8tbsp (½ cup/100ml) bleach, 2oz (¼ cup/60g) baking soda and 1½pt (4 cups/1l) warm water. Apply with a sponge, leave for 10min, rinse off and dry well.

Dry eggshells, crush them, add a little salt and borax, and you will have an excellent cleaner for removing obstinate stains from enamel and kitchen utensils.

Salt will remove burnt marks from the edges of pie dishes, stains from china and earthenware and egg stains from cutlery.

Treat stains on a laminated plastic surface with undiluted washing-up liquid or a cream bath cleaner. Do not use an abrasive powder. For a persistent stain, try a one-step car cleaner.

Use hot detergent suds to remove grease from kitchen surfaces. Allow to dry, then apply a little silicone cream to paintwork, enamelled surfaces and tiles.

When you spill hot fat on the floor or a wood surface pour on a little cold water immediately. The fat will harden quickly. Scrape it off when set and remove the remainder with hot suds.

Everbody wants to harvest, but nobody wants to plough.

KITCHEN HINTS

Never discard the marble top from an old washstand, it's great for making pastry on.

Grease a new cake tin before use, then bake in a moderate oven for 15min and it will never rust.

Wrap soap pads in tinfoil, keep immersed in a small pot of water or sprinkle a little baking soda in the bottom of the dish in which you leave it, to prevent rusting.

Glycerine makes an excellent lubricant for egg beaters or kitchen utensils with moving parts. Unlike oil, it will not spoil the taste of food if mixed with it accidentally.

Aluminium foil makes a sensible cover for a recipe book that is regularly used.

Cling-film kept in the fridge is much easier to handle.

Keep margarine wrappers and store in the fridge for greasing cooking tins and trays.

To loosen screwtop jars or bottles, either tap around the metal top sharply at an angle or heat the lid under a running tap, to expand the metal. Wind rubber bands around the lid tightly in order to get a firm handgrip.

Line tins and jars with blotting paper to keep biscuits fresh.

If you live in a hard water area, prevent the kettle furring up by boiling 1tbsp (20ml) vinegar in a kettleful of water every week. Rinse well before using again.

If a plastic utensil develops a crack, heat a small screwdriver to medium heat (not red hot), then run it over the crack. This dissolves enough plastic to create a good join.

A loving wife will do anything for her husband except stop criticising and trying to improve him.
J. B. PRIESTLEY

TIME SAVERS

If curtain rails are sticking, give them a wipe with furniture polish and clean off.

Slip a thimble over the end of a rod before threading it through a curtain hem. This speeds up the task and prevents the rod catching in the fabric.

When measuring new curtains for high windows, take a long stick and attach one end of a measuring tape to the top with a drawing pin. This enables you to measure the length without balancing on a chair or table.

Hang some large bulldog clips inside the cupboard doors for holding recent bills, receipts, etc. Saves searching in drawers.

Keep cheap talcum powder by the kitchen sink and sprinkle in lightly to rubber gloves before slipping them onto your hands. They will be easier to pull on and off.

When you empty the pedal bin, fold several bin liners or bags and put them at the bottom, before putting in the one for use. This saves having to look for new liners each time you empty.

Keep a nutcracker handy for removing obstinate screwtops from bottles. It is also useful for turning off water at the main stop tap, which is often very stiff.

Place a smear of cooking oil around the necks of bottles which contain sticky substances like sauce; they will be easier to open.

Treat a new bottle of nail polish by rubbing petroleum jelly inside the top and on the grooves of the bottle for easy opening.

To prevent nail-polish caps sticking, always unscrew the cap when dusting the dressing table.

Place a small button at the end of the sellotape roll, the end will be easier to find and the button easily removed.

A thing of beauty is a joy forever.

Use an old shoulder bag for carrying household cleaning materials from room to room. This is a great help when working up a ladder; very useful, too, as a peg-holder at the clothes line.

Use rubber gloves, or a damp sponge of foam rubber to pick up cotton threads, etc, from carpets or upholstery.

Keep a list, inside your attic door, of articles stored up there; remember to score off any taken down.

Help children distinguish between right and left boots and also recognise their own wellingtons by marking the top inner leg with a piece of coloured adhesive tape.

Make your suitcase easy to identify by fastening a wide strip of brightly coloured sticky tape across the top.

Mark your front door key with a little luminous paint to distinguish it from others on the ring. This will save time fumbling around in the dark.

For Christmas decorations – wash holly leaves thoroughly and leave until completely dry. Dip the leaves in melted margarine and cover with sugar. Dry well in front of the fire for lovely frosted holly.

Make snow for Christmas decorations by using a large handful of soap flakes or powdered detergent, add a little water and whip with a mixer. Put on trees and windows, mirrors, etc. When it dries it looks like real snow and lasts for weeks.

Make matching gift tags for Christmas presents by cutting a square of your gift wrap and sticking it onto a white card.

Time and tide wait for no man.

HANDY TIPS

A few glass marbles slotted into the bottom hem of unlined curtains will make the curtains hang better.

Wash plastic curtain hooks and fitments in warm detergent suds, but place brass hooks or rings in a 1:1 solution of vinegar and warm water for 10min.

Decorative plates in a china cabinet will not fall flat if fitted upright in the grooves of corrugated cardboard.

Place a pad of foam rubber or thick felt under a portable sewing machine or typewriter to reduce noise.

Cut a piece of foam plastic to fit inside the base of an umbrella stand to soak up the drips.

Fold some newspapers into a pad and put under the doormat to catch the dirt. Change regularly.

To stop chairs making dent marks on the floor, stick scraps of carpet or self-adhesive felt under the legs and trim neatly.

A plastic vegetable rack is an ideal container for holding toys, especially little things.

An old spectacle case makes a useful container for scissors, needles, pins, etc, when travelling.

To pack coat-hangers tidily, remove the hooks and pack separately.

Wire coat hangers can be made more firm if two are taped together.

Replace small hoops on coats and jackets with a piece of narrow elastic so that the garment can be hung on any hook.

The sticky residue left behind when pulling off price labels can be easily removed with talcum powder. Sprinkle a little on the sticky area and then rub it away with a dry cloth.

Stubborn marks left on polythene and china by sticky labels can be removed by rubbing on a little wax furniture polish or moistening with nail polish remover.

We know nothing of tomorrow; our business is to be good and happy today.

SIDNEY SMITH

To easily take apart two glasses stuck inside each other, pour cold water into the top one and stand the bottom one in hot water.

To make sticky playing cards easier to handle, sprinkle with talcum powder and then shuffle.

Coat the sticky side of self-adhesive hooks with clear nail polish and they will remain stuck. Or try cleaning the area, to which you wish to stick the hook, with pure alcohol.

To prevent sling-back shoes from slipping down, stick a small strip of adhesive foam draught excluder to the back strap.

To undo a knotted necklace chain, place two drops of cooking oil on a piece of waxed paper, lay the knot in the oil and use two straight pins to work it loose. Hang chains and necklaces on hooks screwed inside wardrobe doors.

If the neck of a sweater seems to be high, use one or two clip earrings or cuff-links to keep it folded over.

If you have a friend in hospital and you don't know what to take her when visiting – try a drum of refreshing face-wipes, or nail polish, remover and emery boards.

Keep a pad and pencil by your bedside lamp. It's very useful if you want to make a note for the following day.

The power of appreciating is worth any amount of the power of despising.

HELPFUL HINTS

When fastening a brooch to a coat or frock, sew it on with a few stitches. You'll not lose it even if it comes undone.

If your pretty brooch doesn't have a safety chain, put the pin through a plastic earring keeper and then fasten it. The pin won't slip open.

Before wearing a new garment with buttons, put a little clear nail varnish on the threads of each button to help them stay on.

Keep a pair of cut-off shirt sleeves in the car. If you have to lift the bonnet and tinker with the engine, you can slip these over your arms and keep your clothes clean.

Before putting a suitcase away – rub it over with wax furniture polish, especially the locks and zips.

When lending cups or dishes to someone for a party, put a dot of nail polish on the underside for easy recognition.

If you haven't a telephone, keep a list of important telephone numbers together with some 10p pieces in case of emergency.

Keep a plain candle handy for inked addresses on parcels and plant labels in the garden. Simply rub it over the writing and it will stop the ink smearing. Or cover with strips of Sellotape.

As a collection of addresses is difficult to replace, duplicate your address book and keep it safely at home.

To stop a shoulder bag slipping down your arm, sew a small button under the collar and the strap will stay behind it.

Wet cotton-wool will pick up every fragment of broken glass or china, saving cut fingers.

To make ladders or household steps safer, paint each step or rung, then sprinkle it with coarse sand while still wet. The sand should stick and make the surface non-slip.

Most of the things said about anyone are untrue.

Fasten a pad on the garage wall near the driving seat to prevent scratching as the car door is opened.

Stop car door locks freezing by covering them with sticky tape.

To avoid hitting the facing wall when putting the car into the garage, hang a table tennis ball from a suitable place on the ceiling of the garage, then, when the ball touches the windscreen you know to stop.

Keep the doorstep free of ice by adding ½ cup (125ml) of methylated spirits to 1gall (4.55l) of water when cleaning the steps.

Paint a white strip on the edge of your outdoor steps. This helps you to see them clearly in the dark – especially useful for the elderly.

A foolproof method to secure your door is a wooden wedge pushed in under it.

If you have a security chain on the door, place a small mirror on the wall where the door opens. Fix it at an average person's height so that the caller can be seen in the mirror when the door is opened with the chain on.

To help young children find you on the beach, tie a coloured balloon to your deckchair.

If young children are always playing with the piano, stick a small cork at either end of the keyboard to prevent the lid dropping on their fingers.

The easiest way for your children to learn about money is for you not to have any.
KATHERINE WHITEHORN

Zoe Shorr

CLEANING AND STAINS

❋ ❋ ❋

Housework is a dreadful chore,
Its repetition is a bore.
Many of us tend to complain,
About the chaos of our domain.

    Still

How often do we make a stand,
Refuse to work or lift a hand.
Instead we do the daily grind,
Pretending we don't really mind.

    Still

All we want is appreciation,
For our effort and dedication.
Or better still, flowers sent,
With a precious compliment.

MARY ROSE

UPHOLSTERY

When trying to remove a stain it is necessary to know three things –

the type of material in which the stain occurs;
the nature of the stain;
the properties of the solvents used to remove them. To avoid permanent damage, always test the solvent on an area that won't show, before tackling the stain.

When washing upholstery with detergent, use the lather only. Overlap each section as you proceed and rinse well with a clean damp cloth.

Clean velvet or corduroy upholstery by wiping with a clean chamois leather wrung out tightly in cold water. Treat any stains with dry-cleaning fluid.

Remove spots from Dralon velvet by wiping gently with a cloth moistened with a solution made from a dessertspoonful (10ml) of vinegar and ½pt (275ml) of water. Rinse with clear water.

Use shaving cream as an upholstery cleaner for new stains and ordinary dirt. Or mix ½ cup (125ml) of mild detergent with 2 cups (500ml) of boiling water. Cool until it gels, then whip with a hand beater for a good stiff foam.

Treat a fresh oil or grease stain on upholstery by sprinkling with talcum powder, cornflour or fuller's earth. Rub well and leave until the stain is absorbed. Brush off and wipe with a damp cloth.

Clean vinyl upholstery with a rough damp cloth (eg, old curtain net) sprinkled with baking soda or vinegar. Then wash with mild soap and warm water, rub dry. Never oil vinyl or it will go hard.

To remove felt-tip pen marks from vinyl furniture, tackle immediately with warm water, soap or detergent and a nailbrush.

On an old stain, or if the vinyl is worn, use an abrasive cleaner and camouflage with a matching wax crayon.

An error gracefully acknowledged is a victory won.

CARPETS

Sprinkle a light coloured fur rug liberally with dry powdered magnesia or talcum powder. Rub in well with a clean cloth and leave for a few hours. Beat thoroughly outdoors, shake and remove all powder with a clean brush.

Lay a stair carpet with a spare fold at the top and bottom, so that you can move the carpet up and down a few inches a year. This helps to distribute the heavy wear on the edges of the treads.

Ensure that the pile lies down the stairs and never turn the carpet the other way round.

Always use a carpet liner under a light-coloured carpet before laying it on a wooden floor. This prevents dust rising through the floorboards to the surface of the carpet.

Do not vacuum a new wool carpet for about six weeks to allow the pile to settle down. Use a hand brush or carpet sweeper to remove any excess fluff.

Keep carpets in good condition by vacuuming them at least once a week, and more often in frequently used areas. Remove all stains and spills immediately. Wet clean when necessary, but generally not more than once a year.

After sweeping or vacuuming an old carpet, rub over the surface with a cloth squeezed out in a mixture of one part vinegar to three parts water. This brightens faded colours.

If moths get into a carpet, spread a damp towel over the area and iron it dry with a hot iron. The heat and steam will destroy the worms and eggs.

If a wool carpet has become dented with heavy furniture, place an ice cube or 1tbsp (20ml) water in each dent. When dry, vacuum thoroughly and the pile will spring up like new.

To help make a hearth-rug sparkproof, sponge occasionally with alum and water, using 1tsp (5g) alum to ½pt (275ml) of warm water.

The more we work, the more we may;
it makes no difference to our pay.

CARPETS

To remedy cigarette damage on a wool carpet, remove the charred tips with your fingers. A solution of 3% hydrogen peroxide applied to a light coloured carpet removes discolouration.

Rub a ballpoint pen stain on a carpet with a little methylated spirit on a clean white pad. Sponge with warm water several times and blot dry.

Fresh beer stains should be treated with a squirt of soda water, or sponge with clear, warm water. Blot well and treat any remaining stain with carpet shampoo.

To remove chewing gum from the carpet – apply ice to harden, pick off the gum, then use white spirit or methylated spirit for the residue. Rinse with cool water and blot dry.

Mop up spilt coffee immediately, then rub the area with warm water containing carpet shampoo or washing-up liquid. Or sponge with a solution of baking soda and water. Rinse with cold water. When dry, finish off with dry-cleaning fluid. Shift a dried coffee stain with one part glycerine to one part warm water.

Use baking soda or cornflour to remove small grease marks from a carpet. Pour generously over the spots, then brush lightly through the pile of the carpet. Leave overnight and vacuum next day.

An orange squash stain can be removed by dissolving one dessertspoonful (10g) of borax in ½pt (275ml) warm water. Sponge the stained area, but don't overwet the carpet. Follow with carpet shampoo if necessary.

If you spill red wine or dark sherry on a light coloured carpet, mop with white wine immediately to counteract the stain.

Treat spilt soot on a carpet by covering it with salt. Brush with a stiff brush and repeat the process until the stain has disappeared. Never wet a soot stain.

Opportunities are usually disguised as hard work, so most people don't recognise them.

ANN LANDERS

FURNITURE

Heavy furniture, difficult to move on a polished floor, can slide easily if soft dusters are placed under the legs. To move a side board or flat-bottomed wardrobe, ease up one side and roll a broom handle underneath, then it will move without much effort.

Use a paint brush sprayed with furniture polish when dusting wickerwork. Clean by washing with warm soapy water, then rinse with cold salted water. Dry outdoors when possible.

Use a soft brush dipped in cold salt water to clean bamboo furniture. Dry with a soft cloth, then wipe over the surface with a little linseed oil.

Tighten up sagging cane seats of chairs by scrubbing both the top and underside with hot soapy water. Rinse in cold salt water.

Furniture takes a more brilliant shine if rubbed over with vinegar before polishing.

Use cold tea when cleaning varnished woodwork or floors, and polish with a soft duster. The tannin helps to counteract grease and enhances the wood colour. Good for removing fingermarks.

Slight scratches on furniture can be repaired by rubbing them with a freshly cut Brazil nut – walnuts are also good.

Remove a heat mark from a polished oak table with a half and half solution of turpentine and linseed oil. Dip a cloth in the mixture and rub gently over the white stain. Polish when dry.

To remove water stains from polished wood, smear olive oil or vegetable oil around and over the stain and then, using a generous amount of cigarette ash, rub to a paste with oil. If it's an old stain, leave overnight, if not, then wipe clean and polish.

Candle grease on a wooden surface can be removed by softening with a hair-dryer, then remove with a paper towel. Wash with a solution of vinegar and warm water, dry and polish.

Pride and grace never dwell in one place.

CONCOCTIONS FOR CLEANING

Make an economical window-cleaning liquid by mixing together equal quantities of methylated spirits, paraffin and water. Store in a polythene spray bottle and shake well before use.

A non-slip polish for linoleum can be made by mixing 1tbsp (20ml) paraffin with 1pt (500ml) of tepid water. Apply with a soft cloth and leave to dry completely before walking on floor.

Alternatively, put 1 cup (250ml) paraffin, 1pt (500ml) warm water and 2tbsp (40ml) milk into a bottle and shake well for an economical linoleum polish.

Home made polish –

> 8tbsp (160ml) linseed oil,
> 8tbsp (160ml) turpentine,
> 4tbsp (80ml) methylated spirit,
> 4tbsp (80ml) vinegar.

Put all the ingredients in a bottle and shake well. Use sparingly, leave for a few minutes and polish with a soft duster.

Liquid furniture polish – mix two parts boiled linseed oil with one part each of methylated spirit, turpentine and white vinegar. Store in a firmly corked bottle and shake well before use.

Blanket shampoo –

> 8oz (225g) soap flakes,
> 3 dessertspoons (30ml) eucalyptus oil,
> ½pt (275ml) methylated spirit.

Mix all the ingredients together and use 1tbsp (20ml) to 1gall (4.55l) of water.

There is nothing so easy to learn as experience, and nothing so hard to apply.

METALS

Choose a dry day and polish outdoor brass such as locks and letter boxes, until gleaming, then apply a thin coat of colourless nail polish.

When lacquered brass is looking shabby, remove the lacquer by rubbing with a cloth moistened in methylated spirits. Rinse with warm water, dry and clean with metal polish. Wipe with spirit before applying more lacquer.

Polish brass with olive oil on a soft duster, then rinse off with water and washing-up liquid. Polish with a clean duster.

Lemon juice mixed with metal polish will help to brighten brass and keep it clean longer. Dirty brass can be cleaned by leaving it in Coca-Cola overnight.

Dip a pipe-cleaner in silver polish to remove tarnish from between the prongs of silver forks, clean as usual. Never leave silver standing in a cleaning liquid for longer than 2min.

A few drops of ammonia in the washing-up water will remove the spotty look from silver.

Copper can be cleaned with equal quantities of vinegar and salt. Rinse with warm water and polish with a soft cloth.

To clean copper pans – in a bowl mix four soupspoonfuls (50g) of flour, two egg whites, a small glass of vinegar and a pinch of salt. Rub the copper pans with this mixture, rinse in warm water.

Immerse old and badly stained copper, for a few minutes only, in a solution of powdered toilet cleaner and water. When the copper begins to change colour, remove immediately and rinse thoroughly. Polish as usual.

Use a ball of crumpled silver foil from cigarette packets for cleaning old copper or the chrome parts of a bicycle or pram.

Chrome may be polished with a little baking soda on a damp cloth.

Industry is fortune's right hand, and frugality her left.

WALLS AND FLOORS

If a ceiling is blackened by smoke from the fire, sponge with warm water with washing soda added.

Soot on wallpaper – draw off any surplus with a cycle pump. Brush lightly with soft brush and rub residue mark with a soft rubber.

The smell of smoke is easily removed from a room by burning a few drops of vinegar on a plate or shovel.

Clean varnished wallpaper by wiping over the surface with a cloth wrung out in cold tea, or use 1pt (550ml) of warm water containing 1tbsp (20ml) vinegar.

Use a chunk of white bread to remove finger marks from wallpaper, or to freshen straw hats, fabric lampshades, or light coloured suede handbags, or shoes. Work above a newspaper to catch crumbs.

To remove grease from wallpaper – apply a paste of cornflour and water to the stain. When dry, brush off. Repeat if necessary. Or press the stain with a warm iron over clean blotting paper.

Wash down painted walls with this mixture – add ½ cup (125ml) white vinegar and ¼ cup (60g) washing soda to 1gall (4.55l) warm water. Work towards the floor and wipe each washed area with a clean dry cloth.

A little toothpaste on a damp cloth will help to remove marks on paintwork, especially those made by rubber heels.

Never use wax polishes on vinyl floor-covering, as these soften the surface. If self-shine polishes are used, remove build-up every six months with a recommended solvent.

To remove shoe polish from a tiled floor – mix one part fresh milk with one part turpentine. Rub the mixture into the tiles and polish with a warmed soft cloth.

Practice makes perfect – except when it comes to getting up in the morning.

ROOM FITTINGS

To clean an oil painting, cut a large onion in two. Rub the cut surface on a small area of the painting using a circular motion. As one part is clean move on to the next. When the onion becomes soiled, cut off a slice.

Often wall and grandfather clocks are stopped by dust. Soak cotton wool in turpentine and place it at the bottom of the clock so that the fumes can rise to clean and lubricate the works.

Clean stained cork table mats by wetting the surface and rubbing with pumice stone or coarse sandpaper. Never use soap or hot water. Rinse in cold water and dry in a cool place.

When the artificial coal on the electric fire becomes dull and dusty, give it a light brush with the black shoe brush.

Wash glazed fireplace tiles with soapy water and dry well. Shine with liquid silver polish. This makes the tiles stay clean longer, while the joins will remain white.

After cleaning a fireplace of kiln-dried bricks, paint it sparingly with an equal mixture of raw linseed oil and turpentine substitute to obtain a dirt-resistant finish.

Apply a solution of 1tbsp (20ml) vinegar to 1pt (550ml) water to white patches on quarry tiles. Leave to dry without rinsing. Repeat if necessary and don't polish until patches have gone.

Clean piano keys with a little toothpaste on a damp cloth. Rub the keys well. Wipe dry and buff with a soft cloth. Or clean with a soft rag sprinkled with pure lemon juice.

For stubborn stains on a marble-topped table, rub in a little diluted vinegar or lemon juice, wash off quickly with warm water.

To clean marble, paint the surface with a mixture – one part each of powdered pumice and powdered chalk and two parts baking soda. Leave on for a day, wash off with clean water and a firm sponge.

Books and friends should be few and good.

IN THE BATHROOM

Teach your family that it's easier to clean the bath while it is still warm, and leave a cloth and bath-cleaner near the bath as a reminder. A drop of washing-up liquid in the water helps to prevent a tidemark forming.

For cleaning baths and sinks, use liquid or powdered detergent, as it is much better for the enamel surface.

Treat light stains on a bath by rubbing them with a cut lemon dipped in salt.

For darker stains such as rust, apply a paste of powdered borax and lemon juice, leave for an hour and then rinse thoroughly.

Remove drip marks in a bath by rubbing with warm vinegar, then rinsing thoroughly with hot water. Use daily until the marks disappear, but don't leave the vinegar in contact for too long as it's a corrosive acid.

For persistent yellow stains on a white enamelled bath, apply a paste made from turpentine substitute and baking soda. Leave for a few hours, then rinse off. Repeat if necessary.

To remove a yellowish water mark from the bath – use a mixture of cream of tartar and peroxide. Add enough peroxide to make a paste and scrub the bath vigorously, using a small stiff brush.

Clean and polish a porcelain bath with an equal mixture of raw linseed oil and turpentine substitute. Apply with a soft cloth and rinse off with plenty of warm water. Store mixture in an airtight bottle away from children and shake before use.

To clean a vitreous enamel or porcelain sink, fill with cold water, add a little detergent and household bleach and leave for a few hours.

Everybody's friend is nobody's.

Cleaning Tiles, Taps and Tins

Rinse blotchy bathroom tiles with a cloth wrung out in a mixture of one part warm water to one part vinegar. This removes the hard water deposits. Buff up with a dry cloth.

To brighten bathroom, kitchen or fireplace tiles, wipe down with window-cleaning liquid, then polish with a soft cloth.

Apply a paste of baking soda and water to remove fungus from grouting between wall tiles. Wipe off after an hour with a cloth squeezed out in warm water.

To change your plain bathroom tiles, stick some patterns from adhesive patterned shelf-covering onto various tiles.

When washing tiles in the bathroom, add some perfumed bubble bath to the water. It leaves a lovely delicate smell.

If the mirror backing on bathroom tiles or cabinet starts to come off, leaving ugly brown spots, cut motifs from vinyl wallpaper and stick over the blemish with ordinary glue.

Reduce condensation in a bathroom by running cold water into the bath first.

To shine and remove scum from bathroom fixtures rub them with a cloth moistened with paraffin. Finish off with a dry duster.

Keep chrome taps and towel rails shining by rubbing them occasionally with a cloth sprinkled with a few drops of glycerine – this makes them water repellent.

Remove an accumulation of scale from chrome taps by rubbing with cotton wool dipped in ammonia. Clean and polish chromium plated taps with washing-up liquid.

To prevent cluttering up the bathroom with tins of talc and scent bottles, use a plastic shoe holder and keep them in the pockets.

Hear no ill of a friend nor speak any of an enemy.

IN THE BATHROOM

Cleaning Fittings

Use an old toothbrush for cleaning your combs.

When you pull the plug after washing your hair, place a comb over the hole to catch hair from going down and blocking the pipes.

Sterilise toothbrushes regularly by placing them, bristles uppermost, in warm water containing hydrogen peroxide, for a few minutes.

If a light switch cord becomes discoloured, thread some colourful plastic drinking straws over it.

Clean a plastic light shade by wiping with a damp cloth squeezed out in detergent suds. Dry and polish with window-cleaning preparation. Never immerse the shade in hot water.

Soak discoloured sponges in 1pt (550ml) warm water containing the juice of one lemon. Leave to soak for an hour, then rinse well in clean water.

Face flannels that become slimy due to an accumulation of soap should be boiled in a solution of 1tsp (5ml) vinegar to 1pt (550ml) water for 10min. Rinse in water with a few drops of ammonia and then rinse in clear water. As a preventative, launder flannels in the washing machine weekly.

Rub a grubby cork-topped bathroom stool with fine steel wool dipped in detergent solution. Rinse and dry, then apply a sealer to prevent dirt penetrating the porous surface.

Soak a hardened rubber bathmat for an hour in warm water containing a little glycerine. Rinse in warm water and dry outdoors.

Prevent mildew forming on shower curtains by soaking them in salted water before hanging them for use.

To remove mildew from shower curtains, scrub with a paste of baking soda and water, then rinse.

Sympathy is two hearts pulling at one load.

SHOES ARE MADE FOR WALKING!

New shoes can often cause blistered heels. To solve this problem, rub the backs of the shoes with soap, making them softer.

If new shoes or boots squeak, rub boiled linseed oil into the soles and around the welts.

To make leather shoes waterproof, coat when new with boiled linseed oil. Repeat three times, drying outdoors between rubbings if possible.

Prevent patent leather shoes from cracking by rubbing them occasionally with petroleum jelly, milk or olive oil, then polish before wearing. Store in a warm place, as cold can cause cracking.

Remove scuff marks from patent leather shoes by rubbing with a little egg white. Leave to dry, then polish as usual.

Freshen up gold or silver evening shoes by wiping them lightly with cotton wool dampened with soapy water. Dry and store in dark tissue paper to prevent tarnishing.

Renovate worn suede shoes by holding them over a steaming kettle. Allow to dry, then raise nap with a suede brush.

When cleaning suede, brush over with lemon juice, then steam for a few seconds. Brush with a suede brush.

To clean shoes and put a beautiful shine on them, rub with a banana skin. On brown shoes use the pithy side of a lemon.

When children's shoes are badly scuffed and won't take the polish, rub them with a piece of a raw potato, then apply polish.

After polishing a toddler's shoes spray them with hairspray and the polish won't come off so easily. Or apply nail varnish to places that are frequently scuffed.

If the shoe fits, wear it.

SHOES

Clean white leather shoes, belts or bags by applying a little cleansing milk on a pad of cotton wool. Leave for 10min then polish with a dry duster.

When cleaning sandals or openwork shoes, slip a plastic bag over your hand holding the sandal. This stops your hand being stained by the polish or cleaner.

Disguise a scratch on leather with a matching crayon.

Remove sea-water stains from leather shoes by wiping thoroughly with warm water, then apply olive oil generously. Leave to stand a few days while the oil is absorbed, then polish.

To dry wet shoes, fill them with crumpled newspaper, and wrap each shoe in newspaper. Leave in a warm place so that the paper absorbs the moisture.

Sprinkle a little baking soda in shoes to absorb smells.

Shoe polish that has become hard and dry can be moistened with a little vinegar, a few drops of paraffin, olive oil or turpentine substitute, then place the tin in a warm place a few minutes.

When shoe brushes are caked with polish, soak in warm soapy water containing 1tbsp (20ml) turpentine. Rinse in clean, warm water, then cold; dry thoroughly.

If the ends of shoe laces have become frayed, dip them in nail varnish.

After you've dyed a pair of shoes, give the heels a coat of clear nail varnish. It prevents the new colour scraping off.

Never wear good shoes when you are cooking, especially if they are suede or light coloured – grease is very difficult to remove.

The size of sums of money appears to vary in a remarkable way, according to whether they are being paid in or paid out.

72

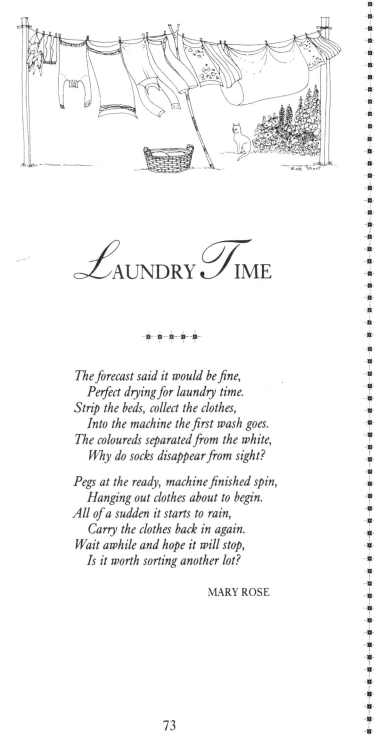

$\mathcal{L}$AUNDRY $\mathcal{T}$IME

The forecast said it would be fine,
* Perfect drying for laundry time.*
Strip the beds, collect the clothes,
* Into the machine the first wash goes.*
The coloureds separated from the white,
* Why do socks disappear from sight?*

Pegs at the ready, machine finished spin,
* Hanging out clothes about to begin.*
All of a sudden it starts to rain,
* Carry the clothes back in again.*
Wait awhile and hope it will stop,
* Is it worth sorting another lot?*

MARY ROSE

WASHING

Put a large polythene bin liner into the linen basket; clothes are easier to lift out on wash day. If it's a wicker basket, this will prevent snagging of delicate articles.

Wear a towelling apron on washdays. To avoid chapped hands, dry your hands frequently and apply handcream liberally when finished.

Never wash pale fabrics with darker fabrics. However fast you think they might be, it's not worth the risk.

To test for colour fastness – wet a corner and squeeze it in a white towel.

Tea towels can be kept in excellent colour by putting the rind of a lemon in the water you wash them in.

Wash nylon sweaters inside out to prevent sagging.

When washing underwear, swish a few drops of your favourite perfume through the final rinsing water – this gives a long-lasting fragrance.

Before washing socks or corduroy clothing, always turn them inside out to avoid picking up fluff.

When children's white nylon socks have lost their freshness, boil them for a few minutes in water containing one or two teabags.

Use an old shaving brush with its soft bristles for painting liquid washing products on badly stained collars and cuffs, before putting them into the washing machine.

The years teach much that the days never know.

Add a couple of sugar lumps to the rinsing water when washing silk to give the fabric more body.

Avoid the grey look to nylon garments or curtains by adding a little vinegar or methylated spirit to the final rinsing water. Rinse 2 to 3 times to remove all traces of soap powder.

Wash fibre-glass curtains gently by hand. Use hot soapy suds and rinse twice in warm water. Wrap in a towel to remove excess water. Rehang while damp, and smooth hems carefully with fingers.

Heavily creased nylon or Terylene can be smoothed by placing the item in water with washing powder. Raise the temperature to very near boiling, agitating from time to time. Remove the garment, immerse in cold water and drip dry.

When washing curtains, mark the position of each hook with felt tip pen on rufflette tape. Replacing hooks will be easier.

Keep your woollens beautifully soft by adding 1tsp (5ml) hair shampoo to the washing water. It improves matted woollens.

Remove unsightly bobbles from wool sweaters and socks by brushing with a wet nailbrush.

When washing woollens, squeeze gently under the water. Don't lift them in and out as this causes stretching. Remove all traces of soap by adding a little vinegar in the final rinse; this keeps woollens soft and fluffy.

When washing blankets put a bath cube in the final rinsing water – it give a lovely fresh smell.

Add a little salt to the final rinsing water before hanging out clothes on a frosty day. This prevents them freezing.

If you accidentally put too much soap powder into the washing machine, put ½tsp (2.5g) Epsom Salts in, to dissolve suds.

Boil discoloured wood pegs in a weak solution of water and bleach for a few minutes. Rinse in cold water and dry out of doors.

Leisure is sweet when it follows work well done.

IRONING

Learn to iron while sitting down, and save your legs. If you prefer to stand, slip off your shoes and stand on a large soft cushion, which will ease your feet and prevent tiredness.

Ordinary tap water may be used in a steam iron if 1tbsp (20ml) ammonia is used to each cup of water. Ammonia softens the water. Ammoniated water also makes for smoother ironing.

Use melted ice from the fridge tray as sterilised water for your steam iron.

After filling a steam iron, wait until it has reached the pre-set temperature before using, or it may drip and leave a water mark on the fabric.

Keep a small piece of damp sponge handy when ironing. When there is a dry crease, rub the sponge over it and the fabric will be lightly and evenly dampened.

If the base of your iron is stained or sticky, unplug and rub with a cloth dipped in vinegar or methylated spirit.

To prevent an iron from sticking to soft silky fabrics, sprinkle a soft rag with talcum powder and rub the base of the iron with it occasionally.

To clear a clogged iron, use 1 cup (250ml) vinegar instead of water and steam until the jets release.

Remove brown stains from the base of iron with a soap-pad.

To iron pleated skirts easily and quickly, fix pegs to the bottom of the pleats.

To press a jacket sleeve without making a crease, roll up a thick magazine, cover with a cloth and insert it into the sleeve. It will immediately unroll and make a firm ironing pad.

Nowadays women don't hire domestic help – they marry it!

Trouser creases stay in the right place when you rub them on the inside with a piece of wet soap. Then iron on the right side.

To remove shine from trousers or skirts, sponge the affected areas with a weak solution of ammonia (1tsp (5ml) per 1pt (550ml) warm water). Press with warm iron using a damp cloth until perfectly dry.

When letting down a hem on trousers or skirt, help to remove the crease mark by rubbing a bar of soap along the line on the inside before pressing.

Another hint to remove the crease mark is to rub the mark with salt on a damp cloth.

After letting down a child's jeans, paint on diluted blue permanent ink to camouflage the white worn line.

After ironing or folding matching sheets and pillow-cases, place the sets of sheets inside the respective cases before you put them away. It saves searching when you require them.

To reduce your ironing load, fold and stack sheets, pillowcases and tea-towels in the airing cupboard; the warmth and weight of the clothes will remove most of the creases.

Tomorrow, tomorrow, not today,
hear the lazy people say.

IRONING

When there's no iron available, remove creases from a garment by hanging it up in the bathroom while you have a hot bath – steam makes the creases drop out.

Before putting on a new ironing board cover, wrap the board surface in aluminium foil. This will reflect the heat and the iron will move more easily over the board.

A newly ironed garment will crease again very quickly, so avoid wearing or packing it for several hours.

When folding garments, make the folds crosswise and not lengthwise where possible. The creases will then drop out more easily when unpacked and hung up.

When packing clothes, fold them over rolled up plastic bags as these stay springy and so help prevent creases.

Discourage moths by having woollens cleaned before storing, wrap in plastic bags, add some cloves or dried orange peel and seal.

Line clothes cupboards and drawers with sheets of white damp-proof paper which can be bought in most wallpaper shops. This will keep clothes damp free and is also moth-proof.

Hang black or navy dresses or skirts inside out in the wardrobe to protect them from dust and fluff.

After washing a sheepskin rug, fluff it with an Afro type comb.

When drying woollies on a line, thread a nylon stocking through the sleeves and fasten the pegs to this.

Get extra space in the airing cupboard by :

> Stretching plastic spring wire across the back of cupboard and doorframe.
> Fixing a pillowcase to the inside of the cupboard door to keep small articles in.
> Screwing cup hooks around the top of the cupboard to hang up blouses or shirts without creasing them.
> Fixing towel rails to the inside of the door and underneath the shelves. You can hang coat hangers on them.

Work expands to fill the time available for its completion.

78

STAINS

Rinse Coca-Cola stains in cold water. Work in liquid detergent from the back of the fabric and rinse. Sponge a persistent stain with methylated spirit plus a little white vinegar and water.

Remove alcohol stains by washing in cool, soapy water with a few drops of ammonia added. Rinse well in lukewarm water.

Treat a chocolate, cocoa or coffee stain on washable fabric by washing in lukewarm soapy water. Rub glycerine into the remaining stain – leave one hour and wash again in soapy water.

To remove coffee, tea or cocoa stains from fabric, stretch the stained material over a small basin, dampen with water, sprinkle with borax, then pour boiling water through. Leave to soak in the solution, then rinse and launder.

Loosen a dried tea stain on a blanket by soaking in a mixture of one part glycerine and two parts water. After 20min wash as usual. Remove a fresh tea stain by soaking in warm water and borax.

Dye stains on white fabric can be removed by dabbing on hydrogen peroxide and drying in the sun. It may take up to three treatments. Alternatively soak the stain in methylated spirit.

Dye dull or faded bed linen with a hot water dye in the washing machine, then run the machine on its hottest cycle with a cupful of bleach in it to clear all the traces of dye.

Restore cream coloured fabric to its natural colour by soaking in strong hot tea. Add a pinch of salt to keep the colour fast.

Yellowing wool can be whitened by soaking in a solution of one part hydrogen peroxide to ten parts water.

There are hazards in anything one does, but there are greater hazards in doing nothing.

STAINS

To remove tar from clothes, scrape off the excess, rub lightly with eucalyptus oil on a cotton wool pad. Keep turning the pad to avoid spreading the mark and work from the outside to the centre. Remove any residual marks with dry-cleaning fluid.

Blue paint brush cleaner will remove oil or tar stains from clothing; very useful for bicycle stains on children's socks. Use neat on wet garments. Rinse off well.

Remove grass stains on a nylon garment by rubbing with glycerine. Leave for one hour and wash out. On other clothing, grass stains can be treated with methylated spirits. Rinse well with warm water.

If jam is spilt on clothes try this remedy – add 2tbsp (40ml) vinegar to 1pt (550ml) of hot water. Dip the stain in this solution, then place the garment on top of a clean folded towel and keep dabbing the stain particularly around the edges.

Soak milk stains in warm water and glycerine, brush lightly and wash as usual.

Vinegar stains on white material should be boiled gently with soap and 1 dessertspoonful (10g) of borax.

To remove a beetroot stain – soak a piece of bread in water and dab it on both sides of the cloth. The bread absorbs the red colour.

When treating a beetroot stain – immediately place the affected material over a bowl and pour boiling water on it from a height.

Soak a tomato stain on washable material in tepid water containing a little ammonia.

Treat mayonnaise stains with glycerine or a dry-cleaning solvent, then wash in tepid water with a few drops of ammonia.

Remove food grease stains on clothing by applying talcum powder immediately to the area, leave to dry for 5min, then brush off.

Alternatively, cover with brown paper and press with a hot iron; the paper will soak up the grease.

If all the year were playing holidays, to sport would be as tedious as to work.

SHAKESPEARE

Sprinkle a grease stain on non-washable fabric with talcum powder and leave for a few hours. Brush off and apply dry-cleaning fluid to remove last traces.

Plunge a fresh gravy stain on washable fabric into cold water first, then treat with a dry-cleaning fluid because the staining ingredient in gravy is often grease-based. Launder as usual.

Remove a grease line from a shirt collar and cuffs by rubbing heavily along the mark with ordinary chalk. Leave overnight and the dirt will come out in the wash.

To remove ballpoint pen marks on clothes or bed-linen - apply methylated spirit, or rub the mark with white toothpaste, leave a few minutes and wash off.

To remove a ballpoint ink mark from cloth, rub a paste of baking soda and milk over it. Rinse, then wash normally.

Soak ink stains on coloured washable material in milk (sour if possible) or in a 50:50 solution of white wine vinegar and water. Rub ink stains on white material with a cut lemon, sprinkle with salt and leave for an hour. Launder as usual.

To remove an old ink stain from a white tablecloth – dip in cold water, then cover stain with a paste of cream of tartar and lemon juice. Leave for an hour, rinse thoroughly and launder as usual.

Soak a fresh bloodstain on washable fabric in cold salted water.

Soak a dried bloodstain in a solution of one dessertspoonful (10ml) ammonia to 1pt (550ml) water for several hours. Launder in warm suds.

Egg-white removes chewing gum from washable fabrics. Apply when the gum is soft, pick off as much as possible and launder as usual. On non-washable fabrics sponge with dry-cleaning fluid.

To remove ironmould stain from linen, cover the mark thickly with salt, moisten with lemon juice. Leave for an hour and then launder.

Keep the eyes wide open before marriage, and half shut afterwards.
BENJAMIN FRANKLIN

STAINS

Remove rust stains by covering with salt and moisten with lemon juice. Leave for half an hour, then wash in a weak solution of ammonia before laundering.

Rust stains on cotton can be moved by adding 1tsp (5g) oxalic acid to 1pt (550ml) hot water. Sponge the stains. After a few minutes rinse thoroughly in clean water. Wash as usual.

Apply diluted ammonia to fresh perspiration stains or white vinegar to an old stain and rinse before laundering. Another solution for perspiration stains is to apply a paste of cream of tartar, three crushed aspirins and warm water. Leave 20min then rinse with warm water.

To remove old urine stains from material, soak the garment for an hour in a mixture of one part hydrogen peroxide to six parts water, with a few drops of ammonia added. Launder as usual.

A good way of removing light scorch marks from white fabric is to place a clean cloth dampened with hydrogen peroxide over the stained area. Cover with a clean dry cloth and press lightly with a warm iron. Repeat if necessary.

Treat a mild scorch mark on washable linen or woollen material by applying a thick paste of glycerine and borax. Leave for an hour, then remove the paste with a blunt knife and launder the garment. Rubbing a slight scorch on suiting with the edge of a silver coin will often move it.

Only a fool tests the depth of the water with both feet.

GARDENING FOR PLEASURE

* * * * *

HOW TO PRESERVE CHILDREN

1 large grassy field
2 or 3 small dogs
some pebbles
a pail of brook
flowers
sunshine

Mix the children and the dogs well together,
    stirring constantly.
Pour the brook over the pebbles.
Sprinkle the field with flowers.
Spread a deep blue sky all over and
    bake in the hot sun.
When brown, remove and set away to cool
    in a bath tub.

FLOWERS

A few drops of household bleach added to the water of cut flowers prevents the water becoming stagnant – and it does not harm the blooms.

Pop a small piece of charcoal in the water when arranging flowers. This keeps the water pure and odourless.

When arranging flowers in a wide-necked vase, stick lengths of sticky tape across to form squares. These will hold the flowers in position.

When arranging flowers with delicate stems, make a hole in the Oasis with a fine knitting needle.

When arranging flowers in a vase, overcome the problem of small or broken stems by slipping them into drinking straws cut to the required length for display.

Pick garden flowers in the cool of the morning or evening, not during the hot part of the day. Choose buds or half open blooms.

Cut flowers will last longer if you cut stems at an angle with sharp scissors. Trim stems under water so that no air bubbles can form to stop the free flow of water into the stem.

To extend the life of tulips, make a series of tiny holes down the whole length of the stems. Wrap droopy tulips in newspaper and plunge up to the necks in water overnight.

Daffodils will last longer if cut above the white stem base and placed in very cold water in a cool place for an hour. Add a copper coin to the water in the vase. Keep away from heat.

Cut anemone stems on the slant, submerge them up to their heads in water for an hour or two until the texture of the flowers is firm. Add 2tbsp (40ml) vinegar to 2 cups (550ml) water in the vase.

There are many beautiful things, but the silent beauty
of a flower surpasses them all.

INDOOR PLANTS

If a pot plant such as a busy Lizzie (*Impatiens*) is flagging, water it everyday with cold tea. The minerals will encourage it to liven up.

Clean mother-in-law tongue (*Sansevieria trifasciata*) by wiping the green foliage every 3 to 4 weeks with a few drops of almond oil squeezed on to a damp cloth. This will ensure glossy green leaves that don't dry up in central heating.

When buying potted chrysanthemums, make sure that there is a fair amount of colour showing through the buds: if you buy them in tight bud they may never open. A well grown plant should have around 20 buds showing colour, with more to come. Water during the first week only if the soil seems really dry.

Remove the lower leaves and split the ends of chrysanthemum stems before putting them in a vase. Put in a cool place at night to extend their life.

If you have non-flowering houseplants, sprinkle a few seeds of small flowers, such as aubretia around them. Cover lightly with soil or compost and you will have a lovely splash of colour.

To let your plants get water while you are away, try this plan – stand a container of water near the plants. Get some pieces of thick wool and place one end of each piece in the water and the other in each flower pot. The wool will absorb the water which will drip into the pots.

Keep indoor plants growing straight by frequently rotating the pots about a quarter of a turn so they absorb the sunlight evenly. Plants lean toward the strongest light (but do not rotate cacti, such as *Schlumbergera*, once the flower buds have appeared).

Put several eggshells in a jar, fill with water. Allow to stand for a few days. Use this mixture to water indoor plants. Or use the water left over from boiling eggs or flat soda water.

Weeds never take a holiday, nor should hoes.

GARDENING TIPS

1tbsp (20g) Epsom salts dissolved in about 1pt (550ml) lukewarm water is a marvellous tonic for plants, especially roses.

Bury banana skins and crushed eggshells near the roots of rose trees to supply them with extra vitamins and minerals. Garlic grown near roses is supposed to keep them clear of greenfly.

Eggshells ground finely may be used not only as a fertiliser but also as a slug deterrent.

After putting garden waste on a compost heap, cover with a black plastic bag weighed down with stones. This gives the best and quickest conditions for rotting.

Don't throw away those nettles; when they have rotted put them into a bucket outdoors, cover with water, and leave for 2 to 3 weeks. The resulting strongly smelling liquid is an unrivalled fertiliser, especially good for tomatoes.

Use leafmould on your garden instead of expensive fertiliser. Collect autumn leaves in sacks, put a brick on each one and by spring your free leafmould is ready for use.

Use an old bicycle pump as a pest killer spray in the garden.

To get rid of ants in the garden, sprinkle some talcum powder.

Sprinkle salt on paths and brickwork crevices to get rid of weeds and grass. Salt will have the same effect if sprinkled on the roots of weeds in the garden. Sprinkle salt on slugs to kill them.

Spread soot or coal around the lettuce bed to keep off slugs.

Remove green fungi from a cement path or patio by pouring on water containing bleach, then scrub with a brush.

A good gardener always plants three seeds –
one for the grubs, one for the weather, one for himself.

Gardeners will find it very useful if they mark off a long handled garden tool in centimetres and metres.

Remove rust quickly and easily from garden tools with a soap-filled steel-wool pad dipped in paraffin. Finish off by rubbing with a piece of crumpled aluminium foil.

To prevent new wooden posts from rotting in the ground, cover the whole base of each with a mixture of raw linseed oil and powdered charcoal before fixing.

After sowing seeds, pop the empty packet into a glass jar and place it upside down at the end of the row.

Lift and divide most perennials every fourth year, in the autumn.

When starting to garden don't just rely on the information on the seed packets. Invest in a good gardening book and keep a diary on the progress of your plants so that you can rectify any problems in the following year.

If you save tips from papers and magazines, put the date on them so that when you look back at them you will know to which season they refer.

Cut flower preservative:
1tsp (5ml) sterilising fluid, 1tsp (5g) alum, 8tsp (40g) sugar. Add these ingredients to 1gall (4.55l) water. Reduce in proportion for smaller amounts of water. Do not change the water in vase, just top up.

To get real enjoyment out of a garden, put on a straw hat, dress in old clothes, hold a trowel in one hand, a cool drink in the other, and tell the man where to dig.

REDUCE PROBLEMS IN THE GARDEN

Choose new plants wisely and make sure that they are not too tender for the climatic conditions in the area. Check as well that the soil and light requirements are correct.

When buying plants make sure they have abundant roots and sound stems. Do not buy plants or shrubs with brown patches. Avoid container grown plants that lift easily out of their pots.

Prepare the ground thoroughly – poorly drained soil can be the basis of root-rotting diseases.

Plant in the correct way and proper place. This will reduce the risk of problems due to wind-rock, frost damage, poor root development, light deficiency, drought or water-logging.

Avoid overcrowding as this encourages mildew and other diseases.

Plants can die due to dry roots at planting time or during the first season in the garden. Water during any dry spells.

Inspect plants regularly to catch problems early. This way a few slugs or insects can be removed by hand or first spots of disease treated with a fungicide.

Spray only when necessary and use the correct treatment.

Provide frost protection if necessary, as frost and snow can cause great damage.

Remember most plants or shrubs need feeding, especially in the early growing season. Check with the garden centre or use a good gardening book for information on feeding.

There are different techniques for pruning plants and shrubs, so again, consult your book.

One year's seed is seven years' weed.

HOME DECORATING, KNITTING AND SEWING

THAT'S NOT MY JOB

There is a story told about four people named Somebody, Everybody, Anybody and Nobody. There was one important job to be done. Everybody was sure that Somebody would do it, but Nobody did it. Somebody got angry about it because it was Everybody's job. Everybody thought Anybody could do it. Nobody realised that Everybody wouldn't do it. It ended up that Everybody blamed Somebody when Nobody did what Anybody could have done.

WALLPAPERING

Tie a piece of string or wire across the top of the paste bucket to rest the brush on. It is also useful for removing excess paste from the brush.

When removing picture hooks or screws from the walls prior to re-papering, stick markers in the holes to know where to re-hang.

To remove washable or painted wallpaper more easily, rub over the surface with a wire brush to allow water to soak in.

Add a good tablespoonful (25g) of baking soda to each bucketful of warm water when stripping wallpaper and the task will be easier.

Use hot water containing vinegar when removing wall-paper. Dip a paint roller or a large sponge into the solution and wet paper thoroughly. After two applications the paper should peel easily.

For removing stubborn wallpaper use a mixture of wallpaper paste, water and liquid detergent. The paste will hold the water in place while the detergent speeds up the wetting process.

Newly plastered walls need to be sized before painting or paper hanging. Special size or diluted wallpaper paste can be used.

Note quantities used to decorate a room and jot it on the wall before you finish papering – no need to measure next time.

When patching wallpaper, tear the paper to shape and it will be less noticeable. Match pattern carefully and paste in position.

After papering a room put some left-over paste into a screwtop jar. It will come in useful later if you discover that a piece of wallpaper needs sealing down more firmly.

After wallpapering, rinse the paste table and brushes in salted water before washing. This removes the paste more quickly and leaves the brush bristles soft and springy.

Looking for new ways to do old jobs means progress.

PAINTING

To remove mould or algae on an outside wall, scrape it away with an old knife, then wipe the wall with a solution of equal parts bleach and water. Repeat next day.

Even in dry weather avoid outdoor painting in early morning or evening if there is any likelihood of dew or mist. Any moisture on wood can cause blistering of paint later.

Always buy good quality paint brushes because cheap ones may shed hairs. Soak a new brush in linseed oil for 24 hours before using it for the first time. It will last longer and be easier to clean.

If a paint brush has gone slightly hard, soften it by boiling it in vinegar for 10min. When the bristles are really hard, soak the brush in cellulose thinners in a glass jar overnight. Rinse well.

When filling the cracks in walls before decorating, mix the filler with the emulsion to be used on the walls. These repairs will dry out the same colour and one more coat will make the repair invisible.

When painting a ceiling, make a slit in the centre of a large bath sponge and push the paint brush handle through it. This will prevent drips.

Before painting a door, rub a little petroleum jelly on the hinges and handles. This makes it easy to wipe off paint splashes. Do the same around window panes when painting frames. Or mould aluminium foil over door handles and fittings.

Slide a few sheets of newspaper under the door when painting to catch the drips. Or put newspaper behind pipes when painting them to avoid painting the wall.

Cover the paint tray with aluminium foil or a polythene bag when painting with a roller. This can be disposed of afterwards.

Messy painters should stand the paint pot on a paper plate to catch the drips.

When success turns your head, you're facing failure.

PAINTING

Even when using one-coat jelly paint for woodwork, apply a quick drying undercoat first. This removes the colour of the old paint, fills blemishes and provides a matt surface for the final coat.

If there is only a small amount of paint left over, put it into a small container to prevent it drying up.

To stop a skin forming – pour a little white spirit on top of the paint; lay a circle of foil or wax paper on the surface; stand the closed tin upside down.

Before storing used paint tins, make a paint line around the outside of the tin at the paint level. At a glance you can see the colour and amount left. Keep the tins in a cool dry place.

When you need to touch up small areas of chipped paint, use a cotton bud – no brush to clean.

Use typewriter correction fluid for knocks on enamel fridges, washing machines, or chips on white paintwork.

Dab some paint on a white card to use as a colour guide when shopping for new furnishings.

Use a small foam hair-roller slipped over the end of a large knitting needle to paint behind radiators or awkward places.

When painting stairs, paint every other tread and allow to dry completely before painting the alternate ones. This enables you to use the stairs all the time.

Start at a corner near the window when painting a ceiling. Work in strips parallel with the window. Leave a ragged edge to each strip and overlap well to avoid a hard straight line.

After a painting session, don't wash out the brushes if using them the next day, instead put them in a polythene bag, tie tightly around the handles and stand the bristles downwards in cold water. Alternatively wrap tightly in aluminium foil.

Use paraffin for cleaning paint brushes. It will separate from the paint afterwards and can be drained off and re-used. Remove the brush from the paraffin and wash in soapy water. Dry well.

The shortest way to do many things is only to do one thing at once.

With expensive brush-cleaning liquids, allow the sediment to settle at the bottom of the jar, pour off the clear liquid and re-use.

Rinse washed paint brushes in a little fabric conditioner to make them soft and like new. Try combing them with an old comb.

After cleaning brushes, keep them in good shape by putting an elastic band around the tip of the bristles. Remove when dry.

Avoid getting paint on your hands when cleaning paint brushes – put a spoonful of brush cleaner into an unperforated polythene bag, put the soiled brush in and work the cleanser into the bristles from the outside.

Cover your hands with plastic bags to avoid getting paint drips.

Window-cleaner will remove paint from your hands and isn't usually as smelly as white spirit. Another method is to spray the hands with furniture polish and wash off with washing-up liquid.

Wipe up spilt emulsion paint immediately with a damp cloth or it will harden and become permanent. Sponge with cold water and keep rinsing until most of it has disappeared. Finish with a dry-cleaning fluid.

To remove the smell of paint from a newly decorated room, cut an onion in half and leave in the room. The smell will disappear.

If you tell a man there are 300,000 million stars in the universe, he'll believe you. But if you tell him a bench has just been painted, he has to touch it to be sure!

KNOW YOUR PAINT

Ceiling distemper: for use on ceilings. Not washable.

Oil bound water paint: use on indoor walls and ceilings. This is a washable paint.

Plastic emulsion paint: this gives a hardwearing and washable surface. It dries quickly, does not leave brush marks and is easy to use with a roller.

Flat oil paint: has suede and eggshell finishes and is especially suitable for kitchens and bathrooms.

Semi-gloss paint: an undercoat for gloss paint.

Gloss paint: very hardwearing paint for inside or outside. Tends to leave brush marks unless used carefully. For best results use undercoating.

Enamels and synthetic lacquer paint: these give a gloss finish, are quick drying and leave no brushmarks. Use generally on small areas as they are expensive.

Jelly paint: has a gloss finish and is non-drip.

Rubberised paint: especially made for kitchens or bathrooms as it has a steam-resistant finish.

One-coat paint: no primer is required if painting on hardboard. It can be used over wallpaper or any flat paint.

QUANTITIES

1qt/1200ml undercoat covers about 240sq ft (22sq m)
1qt/1200ml emulsion covers about 200sq ft (18.5sq m)
1qt/1200ml priming paint – approximately 130sq ft (12sq m)

As a cure for worrying, work is better than whiskey.
THOMAS A. EDISON

D. I. Y. HINTS

Puff a little powdered graphite into a jammed or stiff lock. Keep all locks running smoothly by using graphite every six months. Avoid using oil, which tends to gum up the works of a lock.

Before inserting a large nail in wood that may split, first make a starting hole with a small nail then extract it. Dip the large nail in paraffin or rub with soap and it will go in smoothly.

To put a screw in an awkward place, stick a small piece of Blu-Tack on the screw head. The screwdriver will stick to it and make the task easier.

Before fixing screws into wood, rub them with a little petroleum jelly to make them easier to remove later if necessary.

Tip the head of a painted-over screw with a red hot poker. This removes the paint and expands the metal. When it cools, it will come out easily.

Loosen tight screws in wood by dripping a little vinegar on their heads. When the vinegar penetrates the threaded sections, they will be easier to unscrew.

To remove a tight Rawlplug, put a fairly tight screw in about halfway, then pull screw and plug out with pliers.

A saw cuts more smoothly if the cutting edge is rubbed with soap.

When drilling hard metal, instead of oil add a drop of turpentine to the drill point for lubrication.

To stop a drill sliding over and scratching ceramic tiles, stick a piece of plaster tape on the tile and drill through it. Try this when knocking a nail into plaster too, for less chipping.

Keep a few mothballs in the toolbox. They help absorb damp and prevent metal from rusting. A magnet is also useful to keep small screws together.

Talk to a man about himself and he will listen for hours.

D.I.Y. HINTS

When working near baths or sinks, cover with an old sheet in case you drop in something that might chip them. Put in the plug so that small screws or nails don't go down the waste pipe.

Repair a cracked sink temporarily by sticking strips of linen tape or heavy duty waterproofing tape to the outside then cover with two coats of gloss paint.

When using a wheel glass-cutter, dip in paraffin between cuts.

When filling cracks in cement, use a small plastic bag with the corner cut out and pipe in the cement for a smoother finish.

Avoid lumps when mixing plaster by adding plaster to water not water to plaster. Slow up hardening by adding a little vinegar.

When putting adhesive covering on a worktable, wrap a piece of cloth around a rolling pin and use it to smooth out the bubbles.

Before laying cork, plastic or linoleum tiles, warm them gently in a very cool oven. Tiles are brittle when cold and break easily or split when being cut to fit.

When laying linoleum or vinyl, use Plasticine to take an impression of any awkward part around door frames. Draw round this pattern on the linoleum for a perfect fit. Sprinkle talcum powder on the Plasticine and it won't stick to the wood.

After laying linoleum, leave it loose for a few weeks to allow for stretching. Vinyl however, may shrink, so allow an overlap.

When the edge of newly-laid linoleum or vinyl is raised up, place a filled rubber hot water bottle on it. The warmth softens the covering enough to make it lie flat.

To lift a damaged vinyl tile, lay aluminium foil over it and apply a hot iron; the tile will soften and be easier to pull up.

The time to repair the roof is when the sun is shining.
JOHN F. KENNEDY

KNITTING

Use a loose-leaf ring binder to keep knitting patterns in.

When knitting a complicated pattern, sometimes it's easier to copy the basic pattern onto a separate page.

A plastic toothbrush container is a perfect size for storing crochet hooks or cable needles.

Cover an empty kitchen-foil cardboard roll with shelf adhesive covering. Close one end and use as a knitting needle holder. Or slot needles into a piece of curtain tape.

Mark off one knitting needle in inches and use as a tape measure.

When undoing wool from an old garment, wind it round a filled hot water bottle. The wool should have no kinks and be easier to knit.

Put mohair or angora wool in the fridge to cool before knitting. Keeps the fluff down.

Before knitting with white wool, dust hands with scented talcum powder. This keeps the work clean and gives the finished garment a fragrant smell.

To avoid eye-strain when knitting dark-coloured wool, cover your lap with a white cloth.

When starting to knit a garment, leave at least 8in (20cm) of wool and use this to start sewing seams with. Stops seams becoming undone at the bottom.

If the tension of knitting is rather tight and the stitches difficult to slide off, put a spot of polish on a cloth and pull the needles through it a few times.

Instead of joining wool by tying knots, thread one end of the wool through a darning needle and weave it into the end of the new ball for 2-3in (5 to 7cm). This makes a neater and stronger join.

To know if there is sufficient wool to complete another row, the wool must equal three times the width of the work.

Men make houses, women make homes.

To stop the edges of knitting rolling inwards, knit the first stitch of every line. Also makes sewing up easier.

If you tend to cast-off too tightly, try using a larger needle at this stage.

When knitting bands for the edge of a cardigan, use two balls of wool and knit both edges at the same time. Mark button spacing.

When sewing up knitted garments, tack in place with pins with large coloured heads. They're more easily seen in the wool.

Use embroidery thread of a matching colour to sew up knitted garments. This gives neater seams, less sagging and lasts longer.

When knitting children's garments, line the elbows with pieces of nylon. Gives a much longer wear.

If you have problems getting buttons to match knitted cardigans, buy some small curtain rings and crochet round them with matching wool.

When making up a round-neck sweater, sew a few stitches of different coloured wool on the inside back of the neck.

After completing an Aran garment, fold it neatly and sit on it for about half an hour. This gives a natural pressing and improves the finished look.

If knitting squares for a patchwork cover, knit the first square and then join the next colour and proceed with the next square. Join the strips of squares to complete.

It's today's thrift that makes tomorrow's annuity.

SEWING

Stop a thimble from slipping – put some Blu-Tack inside and see the difference.

Stick a small cork on the side of the sewing box to hold the thimble when not in use.

Sew a paper clip carefully under the zero mark on a tape measure; it will be easier to clip onto work for accurate measurements.

Keep a box of paper clips in your sewing box. They're easier and quicker to use than pins when turning up hems on nylon or net.

Keep cotton reels tidy in the work basket by threading them onto a knitting needle and fixing a cork on the end.

Don't stick needles through cotton reels, instead stuff the centre of the reel with a piece of foam and stick the needle into that. Or keep a magnet on the table to rest the needle on.

A needle can be threaded more easily if a little hair lacquer, starch or beeswax is put on the end of the thread.

Sharpen a machine needle by sewing through a piece of sandpaper.

To stop a needle from breaking when sewing thick material, rub grease down the seam.

For a needle threader, use fine fuse wire bent into a small loop.

After oiling a sewing machine, place two thick sheets of blotting paper under the needle and stitch through several times, to absorb the surplus oil.

Keep old mascara brushes and wash well. They are useful for cleaning the sewing machine.

Use a feather instead of a brush for removing fluff and dust from around the spool or bobbin of a sewing machine.

A stitch in time saves nine.

SEWING

After cutting buttons from old garments, fasten together with a piece of thread before putting into the button box. You can see at a glance how many you have of a particular kind.

When dressmaking, press open the seams of garments with a dampened length of ribbon or tape. This way you'll see if the seams are completely open and the rest of the garment won't get damp.

Use a stiff-bristled nail brush to remove cut threads when unpicking stitches from material. It will prove much quicker than fingers or tweezers.

When making buttonholes, moisten the edges with colourless nail polish. When it dries the buttonhole stitches can be made neatly.

Before machining a zipper, Sellotape it into position, stitch through the Sellotape and remove afterwards.

If a zip tends to unfasten, sew a dress hook above it, then slip the tab opening of the zip over the hook. If it tends to stick, rub the teeth with a pencil.

When sewing very fine materials, place narrow strips of tissue along the seams. This keeps the material in place and is easily removed.

Before sewing leather patches or binding on coats, follow round the edges of the patch or binding with the sewing machine, using a large, unthreaded needle. The ready-made holes make sewing easier.

When patching children's jeans, sew up the back pocket and take a piece of material from inside the pocket.

Keep a piece of chalk beside the sewing machine and, should an oil spot get on any material, just rub the area with chalk and leave for a few minutes. Brush off and the spot will disappear.

Measure thrice before you cut once.

Health, Beauty and Public Speaking

HAPPINESS CUP

A quarter cup of friendship
and one cup of thoughtfulness.
Stir together with a pinch of tenderness.
Very lightly blend in a bowl of loyalty,
with a cup each of charity, faith and hope.
Be sure to add a spoonful each,
of gaiety and truth that sings,
and also the ability to laugh at little things.
Moisten with sudden tears of heartfelt sympathy.
Heat in a good-natured kettle and serve repeatedly.

Health is Wealth

If you cannot sleep, try elevating the feet by raising the lower part of the mattress. This allows the blood to flow back up towards the heart.

Relieve insomnia by eating a boiled onion at bedtime.

Eat onions with a fatty meal and avert heart trouble. Onions contain a substance that assists the blood's fat-fighting enzymes.

Tarragon leaves are good for the heart, liver and brain.

Bay leaves stimulate appetite and improve digestion.

Overcome flatulence by drinking a cupful of caraway seed tea after each meal.

Parsley acts as a mild laxative, helps the digestion and stimulates the kidneys and bladder.

Overcome constipation by drinking two glasses of warm water every morning. Use wholewheat flour and bread. Eat more salads, vegetables and fresh fruit.

For a refreshing tonic drink in summer, pour boiling water over freshly picked mint leaves and add a little honey. To aid digestion, enjoy peppermint tea instead of coffee after a meal.

Immediately an attack of cystitis starts, drink a tumblerful of hot water containing 1tsp (5g) baking soda each hour for three hours only. This helps to kill germs and reduce inflammation.

Camomile tea helps to relieve nervous tension, or digestive upsets. Gargle with it to relieve mouth ulcers or dry throat. Try it for swollen ankles, insomnia and loss of appetite.

Sage tea is a valuable tonic that stimulates the circulation and soothes a persistent cough. It is believed to ensure a long life.

Early to bed, and early to rise, makes a man healthy,
wealthy and wise.

Drink marjoram tea to relieve coughs, aching muscles, cramp, colic, nervous hysteria and headaches. Add a muslin bag containing marjoram to a hot bath to ease stiffness from over-exertion or rheumatism.

Apple cider vinegar is a safe remedy for many ailments, including indigestion, diarrhoea, high blood pressure and difficult menstruation. Gargling with 1tsp (5ml) cider vinegar in a glass of warm water relieves a sore throat and a tickling cough.

Garlic is antiseptic and helps to keep infections at bay. It reduces high blood pressure and eases coughing in bronchitis, asthma and whooping cough.

Soothe a troublesome cough with a bedtime drink of hot milk containing a large teaspoon (6ml) of black treacle or molasses and a sprinkling of nutmeg.

If suffering from bronchitis, always warm the bedroom for at least half an hour before going to bed if your home is not centrally heated. Going from a hot room to a cold one can trigger off an attack of coughing.

Place some chopped onion, 1tbsp (20g) demerara sugar, 1tsp (5ml) each of lemon juice and honey in a bowl. Cover and leave overnight. Sip 2tsp (10ml) when necessary for a troublesome cough.

Chew pieces of raw onion to relieve a bad cold or sore throat. Onions can destroy germs in the mouth within 5min.

For a sore throat, gargle with a glass of warm water containing ½tsp (2.5g) each of baking soda and salt.

Unsalted water in which potatoes have been boiled is a soothing cough medicine. Drink it slowly while still warm.

Encourage an asthmatic child to blow soap bubbles. Blowing and taking deep breaths helps to extend the chest cavity.

If you want to be the picture of health you'd better have
a happy frame of mind.

Drink raspberry leaf tea before and during a confinement to help stimulate contractions and ease labour. Use 1tsp (5g) of dried leaves to a teacup (6fl oz/180ml) of boiling water. Use cold raspberry tea as an astringent lotion for the skin.

Rub fresh sage leaves on your teeth to clean them and remove stains. Use sage tea as a mouthwash if you suffer from mouth ulcers, sore tongue or bleeding gums.

Whiten your teeth by brushing occasionally with salt; also good for firming the gums and keeping them healthy.

Treat a chilblain by rubbing it twice daily with a cut onion, dipped in salt. Relieve itching between the toes by rubbing with a slice of onion.

For an attack of hiccups, try sucking a lump of sugar or swallow 1tsp (5ml) vinegar.

Treat minor burns with Milk of Magnesia, or a paste of water and baking soda, or try golden syrup. All of these are reputed cures but always get medical attention for deep burns.

A simple way to ease sunburn is to grate a raw potato. Insert between a piece of gauze or a clean handkerchief and apply to the affected area. It's very soothing and healing.

Remove a bee-sting with your clean fingernail or the blunt edge of a knife. Avoid squeezing the skin, as this expels more venom into the tissues. Apply cold water pad or an ice cube.

After removing sticking plaster, remove the sticky mark by coating with petroleum jelly and leaving for a few minutes before rinsing off. Another method is to use cotton wool dipped in surgical or methylated spirit, or nail varnish remover.

What is an adult? A child blown up by age.

CHILDHOOD INFECTIONS

Measles

Incubation Period: 8 to 10 days before the running nose and head cold, 14 days before the appearance of the rash.

Early Symptons: starts with running nose, bleary eyes and a hard cough. The doctor will look inside the mouth for white spots (Koplik's spots), which appear 2 to 3 days before the rash.

Distinctive Features: the rash appears 3 to 4 days after the first symptoms and begins behind the ears, spreads to the face and then downwards to the body and lower limbs. It has the appearance of dark purplish spots, which run together to make blotchy areas. The eyes are always reddish.

Duration: a few days in bed. Return to school in 2 weeks.

Nursing Points: give mouthwashes after food. If there is severe earache or very inflamed eys, then get medical advice.

Prevention: immunisation is effective in about 95% of cases and most doctors advise routine immunisation of children after their first birthday.

Always laugh when you can, it's cheap medicine.

German Measles (Rubella)

Incubation Period: 14 to 21 days.

Early Symptoms: the appearance of the rash is often the first sign though sometimes there can be some throat discomfort and a slight fever. Painful swollen glands at the back of the head.

Distinctive Features: the rash is pink flat spots that merge together to give a 'peach bloom' appearance.

Duration: around 6 days. Stay away from pregnant women.

Nursing Points: sometimes there is swelling of small joints of the hands, but this will subside. Usually quite uneventful.

Prevention: immunise as a child and as the disease is so serious for pregnant women, most girls are offered the vaccine at around 13 years old. Older women, before conceiving, can have a blood test to determine if they are immune or not.

Chickenpox

Incubation Period: 15 to 21 days

Early Symptoms: when bathing or undressing you may notice spots on the trunk.

Distinctive Features: the spots become 'blistery' then yellow and form scabs. There may be several 'crops' of spots.

Duration: 6 days after the last 'crop' the child is no longer infectious.

Nursing Points: keep fingernails short and clean to help prevent child scratching the irritable spots.

Prevention: there is no immunisation against the disease. Avoid contact with an infected person, though it is usually better not to try to protect children from catching it.

Children never put off until tomorrow the things that will keep them out of bed tonight.

Scarlet Fever

Incubation Period: 1 to 5 days. The rash always appears within 24 hours of the onset of the first symptoms.

Early Symptoms: starts with a sore throat and vomiting. The glands in the neck are painful and swollen. The cheeks are flushed and there is a whitish area of pallor around the mouth. There is no rash on the face.

Distinctive Features: the rash consists of tiny spots that feel like sandpaper and turn white when pressed. It begins on the neck and chest and spreads over the whole body. The throat is brilliant red in colour and there may be white deposits on the tonsils.

Duration: the rash disappears within a week with modern treatment. An untreated case may have peeling of the skin. This is not infectious. Return to school after treatment.

Nursing Points: mouthwashes are soothing and older children may gargle. Report to the doctor within a day or two if you suspect scarlet fever. He may prescribe antibiotics to help prevent complications. Report persistent earache.

Prevention: there is no effective immunisation against scarlet fever.

Mumps

Incubation Period: 14 to 28 days.

Early Symptoms: generally off-colour for a few days before complaining of pain or soreness when chewing.

Distinctive Features: the salivary gland below the ear and behind the angle of the jaw is swollen and painful to press. The gland on the opposite side may be the same up to 7 days later. Boys after puberty may develop painful swelling of the testicles.

Duration: no need to confine to bed unless feeling very unwell. Can return to school after swelling has gone down.

Nursing Points: cleanse the mouth well after meals.

Prevention: there is no means of prevention apart from avoiding contact.

A merry heart kills more microbes than medicine.

Whooping Cough
Incubation Period: 8 to 14 days.

Early Symptoms: starts with 'chestiness' and a simple cough. This becomes spasmodic with a fit of coughing that ends with a whoop and/or vomiting.

Distinctive Features: the diagnosis is obvious. Fast breathing denotes onset of pneumonia. This may occur early in young children who have not been immunised and may leave permanent lung damage.

Duration: 6 weeks' leave from school would be required after a severe attack. Immunised children usually have a mild dose.

Nursing Points: small infants require special care during fits of coughing and should be lifted out of their cots and held head downwards until the spasm ceases. Older children should be calmed and reassured, but usually can cope themselves.

Prevention: as whooping cough is more dangerous than the immunisation, all children should have a course of three injections in the first year of life, usually given with the diptheria and tetanus vaccine. The doctor will take your family medical history before giving the immunisation.

Worry gives little things big shadows.

ANTI-STRESS TIPS

Make lists – but don't set yourself unrealistic aims.

Work in short bursts – you'll be more efficient and less flustered.

Find some satisfaction in your work at home or job – it lifts emotions and avoids fits of depression.

Have regular breaks, and don't turn that self-catering holiday into hard work.

If you start to 'panic', breathe as slowly and as deeply as you possibly can. It will slow down your body and get those panic symptoms under control.

Find some time for yourself every day, even if it means leaving a chore undone.

Feeling tensed up – concentrate hard on a happy scene – perhaps on the beach.

Stop work an hour before going to bed, preferably with a milky drink. Have a good night's sleep.

Don't bottle up your stress – show your symptoms. Tears actually rid our bodies of impurities.

Don't leave things to the last minute.

Learn to relax. Take a bath, enjoy the silence and lack of pressure.

Take regular exercise – go for a walk.

If you do smoke – try to cut down or, preferably, out.

Eat a healthy diet – eat slowly, relax and enjoy your meals.

Light burdens, long borne, grow heavy.

LEMON IS THE ANSWER

Keep rheumatism at bay – drink plenty of lemonade without sugar.

A throbbing headache is relieved by rubbing the temples and forehead with a slice of lemon.

Equal parts of honey, lemon juice and glycerine, taken frequently, 1tsp (5ml) at a time, will relieve a sore throat.

The juice of a lemon mixed with strong coffee usually cures biliousness.

Pure strained lemon juice will often prevent sea-sickness.

Reduce weight by taking the juice of a lemon in hot water every morning before breakfast.

A cup of cold tea, with a slice of lemon, is a refreshing drink.

Rub corns morning and night with lemon and they will disappear.

If you swallow a fish-bone, suck a piece of lemon slowly, the bone will dissolve.

A little lemon juice in a glass of hot water helps remove tartar (plaque) from teeth. Also good as a mouthwash.

Cure dandruff by rubbing lemon juice into the roots of the hair.

If bothered with freckles, rub a little undiluted lemon juice over them every night and in a few weeks they should start to fade.

To whiten a brown neck, rub with lemon juice after washing.

Get rid of warts by rubbing them daily with lemon.

Lemon juice, rose-water and glycerine in equal parts, make a good cure for chapped hands.

The best eraser in the world is a good night's sleep.

LOOK GOOD AND FEEL BEAUTIFUL

Add 1tbsp (20ml) malt vinegar to the final rinsing water after shampooing brown hair, or use lemon juice for fair hair. The acid removes any traces of soap, puts a gloss on the hair and helps reduce dandruff.

Wear a light sunhat in strong sunshine if hair is colour treated.

Cold tea is an excellent after-shampoo rinse and makes your hair shine and feel soft. Massage it into your scalp and rinse off.

To recondition dry hair – shampoo and towel hair dry, apply mayonnaise and leave for an hour. Shampoo with warm water and add 1tbsp (20ml) cider vinegar to the final rinse.

When dandruff is troublesome, mix together equal quantities of cider vinegar and warm water and apply to the scalp daily.

Lank and lifeless hair may be caused through overuse of a regular shampoo. Residue can build up, so change to a mild, medicated one.

To tighten up bags under the eyes, place a damp used tea-bag over each eye, then lie down and relax for 10min. Remove and splash the eyes with cold water.

Encourage eyelash growth by brushing them each night with almond oil on an eyebrow brush. Use only liquid or cake mascara.

Before sharpening an eyebrow pencil, leave it in the refrigerator for an hour. The wax core will harden and ease sharpening.

Simplest and quickest way to combat brow wrinkles is with soap. Work up an extra thick lather and leave to dry on your forehead. Rinse off and apply moisturiser with an upward, massaging motion.

If troubled by lines or wrinkles – apply a good quality mayonnaise to the face night and morning. It helps fine lines to disappear.

Wrinkles should merely indicate where smiles have been.

Avoid a double chin by sleeping on one pillow only, if you lie on your back. Always keep your head up and your chin forward. Apply cream to your neck lightly at bedtime and slap underneath your chin at least thirty times with the back of your hands. After washing splash your neck well with cold water to firm the muscles.

Use the white of an egg as a face mask – beat until frothy, leave to dry on your skin and wash off with warm water. If your skin is inclined to be dry, add 1tsp (5ml) honey to the mixture.

If you run out of skin cleanser, soak swabs of cotton wool in cold milk to remove make-up. Milk cleans and tones skin effectively.

Add a slice of lemon to ½ cup (125ml) hot milk, leave for a few minutes, strain and throw away the curd. Use the remaining liquid as a skin food for both hands and face at night after cleansing.

To keep your skin soft and young looking, put a handful of oatmeal into water and leave overnight to soak. Strain off the water and keep it in a container. Rinse your face with this liquid every morning and your skin will appreciate it.

Restore the natural pH balance to your skin by splashing your cleansed face daily with warm water containing some cider vinegar. Allow it to dry without using a towel. This treatment is helpful for acne sufferers.

Revitalise tired and blemished skin by having a rub down with sea-salt before a bath. Mix a cupful (250g) sea-salt with enough warm water to make a paste. Rub the paste over your body with a face cloth until the skin tingles. Rinse off the salt in the bath or shower. After drying, apply moisturising lotion.

Prepare your whole body for a golden tan by moisturising all your skin regularly after bathing. Soft supple skin will help reduce flaking and peeling after sun exposure.

Beauty is how you feel inside and it reflects in your eyes. It is not something physical.

When your hands are ingrained with dirt after a heavy cleaning job, massage with 1tsp (5g) sugar and a little cooking oil. Remove with warm water and soap, dry your hands thoroughly and apply a nourishing hand cream or a little glycerine.

Try this hand lotion – blend 2tbsp (40ml) each of rose water and glycerine with ½tbsp (10ml) runny honey and the juice of a lemon. Massage into your hands after washing.

Remove nicotine stains from your fingers by rubbing with equal parts lemon juice and eau-de-Cologne. Rub persistent brown marks with cotton wool dipped in hydrogen peroxide; wash thoroughly.

To strengthen fingernails, buff regularly in one direction only. Add 1tsp (5g) salt to ½ cup (125ml) cold water and hold fingertips in this for 2min, twice a week.

Strengthen brittle nails by eating a square of table jelly daily. Massage lanolin into the base of each nail at bedtime. Soak in a solution of one part cider vinegar to eight parts water for 10min, twice weekly.

Slim down fatty hips with a rolling pin. Roll over each thigh for 3min before a bath.

Thick puffy ankles may be due to poor circulation if there is no medical reason. Avoid prolonged standing, crossing legs and tight shoes. Practise ankle twisting and stretching exercises and walk as much as possible daily. Raise feet when relaxing.

Deal with minor foot blemishes daily. A pumice stone will remove dried, hard skin. Apply foot creams and oils regularly to reduce horny pads on the heel and ball of the foot. Cut toenails straight across and file corners with an emery board.

To soften hard skin on feet and make stubborn toenails easier to cut, add some baking soda to warm water and soak feet in it.

Beauty is only skin deep, but ugliness goes to the bone!

20 WAYS TO LOOK GOOD

1. Make time every day for the things you enjoy and concentrate on them for an hour or two, putting all other problems aside. Relax with music or in complete silence, whichever you prefer.

2. Exercise for 10 to 15min every day and drink six to eight glasses of pure natural water daily.

3. Look at your food intake, check if you are eating plenty of raw fruit, vegetables and fibre foods. Eat fish two or three times a week.

4. Spend one day fasting. Eat nothing, but drink plenty. Choose a day when you will be able to relax and not have to rush around.

5. Get your teeth checked by the dentist. Use dental floss and spend 5min cleaning your teeth, twice daily. You may require a new toothbrush.

6. Go the the hairdresser's and treat yourself to a new hairstyle or at least a trim, shampoo and set, or blow-dry.

7. Steam your face – cover your head with a towel and place face over a bowl of hot water. Do this every few weeks to remove impurities.

8. Ask for make-up advice at the cosmetic counter in department stores, you may even be lucky enough to get a free demonstration.

Personal beauty is a better recommendation than any letter of introduction.

ARISTOTLE

114

9. Keep your make-up fresh all day – apply foundation, powder lightly over the top and then apply powder blusher. For lips, apply lipstick, blot, apply more lipstick, and then blot again.

10. Buy bath and body products to match your favourite perfume. Before applying perfume, rub a very thin layer of petroleum jelly on your skin. Oily skin holds perfume longer than dry skin.

11. Pay attention to your body although covered up in cold weather. Use a loofah on elbows, knees and bottom at least once a fortnight during bath-time.

12. Keep legs smooth by waxing or shaving. Check your stock of tights or stockings.

13. Putting your feet up will help you to relax and improve your circulation. Lie on the floor with your feet on the sofa for a few minutes. Manicure your toenails, and your feet will be more comfortable.

14. Make the most of your appearance every day even if you aren't going out. You'll feel better when you know you look good.

15. Do a stocktake of your wardrobe. Throw away any tatty garments and donate any outfits in good condition to a charity. Some of last year's clothes may be easily updated with the help of jewellery or belts.

16. Freshen up your heavy coats and jackets by having them dry-cleaned. Attend to missing buttons and dropped hems, etc.

17. Dress to flatter your body shape, rather than following the latest fashions. Know which colours suit you best. Polish shoes, bags and belts for that perfect groomed look.

18. Keep the fun going in your relationship. Frequently plan trips with your partner to somewhere special.

19. Join your local library or go to evening classes to improve your brain power.

20. Think positive – don't dwell on your bad points. Make the most of your best features.

Smile, and the whole world smiles with you!

LEMON AND BEAUTY

To bring out the highlights in blond hair, add the juice of half a lemon to the rinsing water when you shampoo. For other shades of hair, make up a mixture of 1tbsp (20ml) lemon juice and 3tbsp (60ml) vinegar and add to the rinsing water.

Get rid of spots by mixing 1tsp (5g) salt with the juice of a lemon and dabbing the affected area with this solution at night.

Face-pack – mix together 1tbsp (12g) of oatmeal with lemon juice to a smooth paste. Clean the face well and apply the pack. Leave for 10 to 15 minutes, rinse off with cool water.

Use 'empty' lemon skins – turn inside out and rub over the knees, elbows and heels to soften hard skin and whiten rough areas.

For dull or dingy teeth, twice weekly, dip the toothbrush in lemon juice, then table salt and brush as usual. Rinse thoroughly.

To remove vegetable stains from hands, rub with a mixture of lemon juice and sugar. Wash in warm soapy water.

A beauty bed-time drink – hot water, honey and lemon juice.

How To Become Beautiful

2 ozs of patience
4 ozs good will
1 cup of kindness
1 pinch of hope
1 bunch of faith

To the above ingredients add two handfuls of industry,
　　One packet of prudence and a little sympathy.
One handful of humility must be added,
　　Plus a jar brimful of the syrup of good humour.
Season the mixture with good strong common sense,
　　And simmer down together in the pan of daily content.

TAKE THE FEAR OUT OF PUBLIC SPEAKING

At some time in our lives most of us must express ourselves in public. To overcome your self-consciousness and lack of confidence you should:

Attend meetings and take note of procedure – who says what and how they say it.

Compare speakers to assess who holds your attention and why.

At some meeting second a proposal of thanks; this only takes a few words and you have crossed the first hurdle.

Your next step is to propose the vote of thanks; this takes a little longer but should still be brief.

When it comes to the time that you are asked to give a talk or make a speech, first of all prepare your talk:

Think about and jot down, in any order, what comes into your mind – how your interest in the subject began, developed, what you learned, what you did, the satisfaction it has given you etc.

Then put these into a logical order and divide into three or four headings.

Think of an introduction to your subject, write down your headings, and any sub-headings to each one, then in your conclusion draw everything together.

You may wish to write out your speech but, if you do, read it until you know it well enough to talk to your audience and not just read from a page.

Time the talk as you read it, and add or deduct as necessary. Remember, it is better to be brief than long and boring, or repetitive.

Finally, check that you haven't too many I's and my's in it, and that the language is simple and easily understood.

The next step is the actual giving of the speech. Some wise person once said that the best way to deliver a talk is to stand up, speak up, and shut up. They are good headings:

Stand up: wear clothes in which you feel comfortable and look well, but will not detract from what you have to say.

While you are being introduced take a few deep breaths, this will help steady your nerves.

If you stand, be erect but not stiff, one foot slightly in front of the other to give you balance.

Look pleasant, and before you begin to speak, look out over your audience to make eye contact. Remember they wouldn't be there if they didn't want to hear what you have to say.

Speak up: talk to the people at the back of the room.

Good clear speech, last consonants of words are important.

Don't speak too quickly or let the ends of sentences fade away.

Sound as though you believe in what you are saying.

Keep your tone pleasant and smile where appropriate.

Look out to your audience without looking at any one person.

Address the chair, any honoured guests, then the audience.

Shut up: when you come to the end make it definite.

Just state what you have tried to say.

Sit down and be prepared to answer questions.

*The shortest distance between two jokes makes
a perfect speech.*

118

General advice: don't fidget or fiddle with papers.

Don't be afraid to make gestures, but don't wave your arms about without purpose.

Don't tell jokes unless you are good at it and they are relevant.

An anecdote to illustrate a point is better.

Don't let nerves worry you. Those who have no nerves are most likely people who talk too much.

$$\mathcal{G}\text{OOD}\,\mathcal{L}\text{UCK!}$$

NOTES

NOTES

NOTES

NOTES

NOTES

$\mathcal{I}$NDEX

125